Anthem Test Papers
11+ and 12+ Verbal Reasoning
Book 1

ANTHEM LEARNING VERBAL REASONING

A comprehensive and practical guide to verbal reasoning, this series is an indispensable tool for pupils looking to clear their 11+ and 12+ verbal reasoning exams. Written by experienced tutors, the **Anthem Learning Verbal Reasoning** series offers extensive coverage of the types of problems featured in examinations, including clear, step-by-step instructions on how to solve them. With its useful tips on how to prepare for tests, as well as its wide range of practice materials, the **Anthem Learning Verbal Reasoning** series is a vital resource both for beginners and experienced students.

The series includes a **How To Do** guide on technique and questions likely to be asked, as well as an array of practice and test papers. The **Test Papers** in multiple-choice format can be used to emulate exam conditions, and offer a wide variety of increasingly difficult problems that will challenge pupils of all abilities. Meanwhile, the **Short Revision Papers** in multiple-choice format can be used to pinpoint weak spots and areas for further work, and are perfect for students looking to top up their skills – and for those with busy schedules.

Designed to instil confidence, the **Anthem Learning Verbal Reasoning** series is ideal for those sitting verbal reasoning exams or looking to hone their communication skills, and will be an invaluable resource for students and parents alike.

PUBLISHED BY ANTHEM PRESS

75–76 Blackfriars Road, London SE1 8HA, UK
or PO Box 9779, London SW19 7ZG, UK

ISBN-13: 978 0 85728 383 2 (Pbk)
ISBN-10: 0 85728 383 9 (Pbk)

This title is also available as an eBook.

Anthem Test Papers
11+ and 12+ Verbal Reasoning
Book 1

John Connor and Pat Soper

ANTHEM PRESS
LONDON · NEW YORK · DELHI

Table of Contents

Introduction

The book comprises ten papers, each containing 80 questions, encompassing the major types of problems found in all verbal reasoning papers. It is not possible to give a 'pass' mark, since a number of variables are always present; however, experience has demonstrated that scores of around 65 out of 80 (80%) will indicate a level required by the vast majority of secondary schools.

It is worth emphasizing that the papers vary in degree of difficulty and that the composition of the papers differs slightly. For example, one might include more vocabulary questions than other papers favouring a candidate with a greater ability in English. Another might include a greater mathematical content favouring a candidate with greater ability in mathematics. Hence, it is expected that there will be a variation in the scores achieved.

The key to success on all papers, however, is to complete the paper. Each paper should be allocated 50 minutes. An essential skill in mastering verbal reasoning tests is the ability to work systematically against the clock. It is important to realise from the outset that the crucial determinant in gaining success is the number of questions answered correctly. That is, in a paper comprising 100 questions, a score of 79 correctly answered questions out of 80 completed is a poorer result than a score of 80 correctly answered out of 100 completed questions. Since time is critical, a candidate must be familiar with the most common questions and must possess a strategy on how best to approach each type.

Anthem Test Papers
11+ and 12+ Verbal Reasoning Book 1
Answer Sheet 1

Please select your answers by filling in the correct boxes.

Name:

1
- spot ☐
- dent ☐
- mark ☐
- badge ☐
- stain ☐

2
- device ☐
- object ☐
- dislike ☐
- condemn ☐
- itemise ☐

3
- swing ☐
- pitch ☐
- rock ☐
- stone ☐
- crag ☐

4
- award ☐
- instant ☐
- present ☐
- donation ☐
- register ☐

5
- chunk ☐
- share ☐
- piece ☐
- sample ☐
- article ☐

6
- volume ☐ | boom ☐
- whisper ☐ | silence ☐
- noise ☐ | uproar ☐

7
- truth ☐ | wisdom ☐
- knowledge ☐ | ignorance ☐
- nonsense ☐ | education ☐

8
- admiral ☐ | follower ☐
- leader ☐ | sailor ☐
- command ☐ | order ☐

9
- work ☐ | holiday ☐
- absent ☐ | gift ☐
- present ☐ | past ☐

10
- fake ☐ | fame ☐
- publicity ☐ | real ☐
- fraud ☐ | dishonour ☐

11
- T ☐
- A ☐
- P ☐
- E ☐

12
- W ☐
- O ☐
- R ☐
- L ☐
- D ☐

13
- B ☐
- A ☐
- R ☐
- E ☐

14
- D ☐
- R ☐
- O ☐
- W ☐
- N ☐

15
- N ☐
- I ☐
- E ☐
- C ☐
- E ☐

16
- UX ☐
- UW ☐
- VW ☐
- VX ☐
- TV ☐

17
- LS ☐
- MR ☐
- NR ☐
- LR ☐
- LT ☐

18
- CE ☐
- CD ☐
- BD ☐
- ED ☐
- CF ☐

19
- YX ☐
- XZ ☐
- YW ☐
- YY ☐
- YZ ☐

20
- MN ☐
- NO ☐
- MO ☐
- MP ☐
- NQ ☐

21
- 60 ☐
- 61 ☐
- 62 ☐
- 63 ☐
- 64 ☐

22
- 280 ☐
- 960 ☐
- 1440 ☐
- 2880 ☐
- 4320 ☐

23
- 18 ☐
- 19 ☐
- 20 ☐
- 21 ☐
- 22 ☐

24
- 66 ☐
- 70 ☐
- 72 ☐
- 19 ☐
- 21 ☐

25
- 792 ☐
- 798 ☐
- 803 ☐
- 805 ☐
- 815 ☐

26
- POLE ☐
- POOL ☐
- PEEL ☐
- PEEP ☐

27
- REAR ☐
- MERE ☐
- RACE ☐
- MARE ☐

28
- REAP ☐
- REAR ☐
- REAL ☐
- LEAP ☐

29
- RAW ☐
- FAR ☐
- FAD ☐
- WAR ☐

30
- DRAM ☐
- DARN ☐
- MOAN ☐
- DOME ☐

31
- P ☐
- F ☐
- T ☐
- Y ☐
- N ☐

32
- T ☐
- E ☐
- H ☐
- N ☐
- M ☐

33
- D ☐
- W ☐
- T ☐
- P ☐
- B ☐

34
- D ☐
- B ☐
- E ☐
- Y ☐
- L ☐

35
- T ☐
- O ☐
- S ☐
- K ☐
- H ☐

36
- WANE ☐
- NEAR ☐
- WEAR ☐
- MANE ☐
- WERE ☐

37
- NONE ☐
- TEAR ☐
- RENT ☐
- RATE ☐
- NOTE ☐

38
- TEST ☐
- BEST ☐
- MUST ☐
- TENT ☐
- TUBE ☐

39
- RIDE ☐
- READ ☐
- DEAR ☐
- DEAD ☐
- RAID ☐

40
- SASH ☐
- PACT ☐
- CAST ☐
- CHAT ☐
- CATS ☐

41
- ALL ☐ | LINE ☐
- END ☐ | TOGETHER ☐
- INK ☐ | LESS ☐

42
- HAND ☐ | FULL ☐
- ADD ☐ | FREE ☐
- CARE ☐ | SUN ☐

43
- CARRY ☐ | ABLE ☐
- NOTE ☐ | ON ☐
- LESS ☐ | BAG ☐

Answer Sheet 1

Please select your answers by
filling in the correct boxes.

44

CUP ☐	FULL ☐
SUN ☐	WEATHER ☐
TEAR ☐	BOARD ☐

45

INN ☐	HIRE ☐
NOT ☐	VISIBLE ☐
BE ☐	HAVE ☐

46

leave ☐	patch ☐
school ☐	thoughtful ☐
eject ☐	damage ☐

47

ruler ☐	actor ☐
judge ☐	play ☐
cruel ☐	whole ☐

48

enjoy ☐	unite ☐
hate ☐	encourage ☐
favourite ☐	lead ☐

49

metre ☐	month ☐
measurement ☐	century ☐
distance ☐	time ☐

50

fruit ☐	jump ☐
gloves ☐	three ☐
two ☐	multiply ☐

51

run ☐
walk ☐
sprint ☐
crawl ☐
jog ☐

52

succeed ☐
precede ☐
achieve ☐
winner ☐
triumph ☐

53

pleasant ☐
lucky ☐
agreeable ☐
looking ☐
enchanting ☐

54

guess ☐
measure ☐
estimate ☐
weigh ☐
approximate ☐

55

slap ☐
pain ☐
strike ☐
punish ☐
whack ☐

56

The lion ☐
lion that ☐
that escaped ☐
escaped was ☐
soon captured ☐

57

is important ☐
important that ☐
members of ☐
of the ☐
the choir ☐

58

After the ☐
the race ☐
race each ☐
each entrant ☐
given an ☐

59

The penalty ☐
award made ☐
the players ☐
players hopping ☐
hopping mad ☐

60

The presence ☐
presence of ☐
boys lowers ☐
standards of ☐
of behaviour ☐

61

R ☐
S ☐
T ☐
U ☐
V ☐

62

C ☐
B ☐
A ☐
X ☐
Y ☐

63

FW ☐
FM ☐
FO ☐
GO ☐
HO ☐

64

T ☐
V ☐
W ☐
X ☐
Y ☐

65

L ☐
M ☐
G ☐
N ☐
K ☐

66

TIDE ☐
SIDE ☐
SING ☐
SINK ☐
SKIN ☐

67

JULY ☐
JUTE ☐
JOIN ☐
JEST ☐
JUST ☐

68

DTGCF ☐
DTGDF ☐
DTGCG ☐
DTHCF ☐
DTKCF ☐

69

IMDJ ☐
IMCT ☐
IMJD ☐
IMCJ ☐
IMCK ☐

70

FDVH ☐
FDUH ☐
FDVG ☐
FDUK ☐
FEUH ☐

71

water ☐	multitude ☐
deluge ☐	flood ☐
ice ☐	drizzle ☐

72

colossal ☐	defence ☐
castle ☐	tower ☐
size ☐	massive ☐

73

music ☐	noise ☐
silence ☐	opera ☐
clamour ☐	study ☐

74

police ☐	parents ☐
honour ☐	order ☐
laws ☐	respect ☐

75

rebel ☐	mutiny ☐
navy ☐	army ☐
sailors ☐	soldiers ☐

76

ALL ☐
ADD ☐
AMP ☐
ARE ☐
AND ☐

77

TOO ☐
ATE ☐
ASK ☐
TEA ☐
EAT ☐

78

SAD ☐
NOW ☐
PAD ☐
WON ☐
CAN ☐

79

PAT ☐
ASK ☐
DID ☐
ANT ☐
SAT ☐

80

PEA ☐
SAD ☐
DID ☐
APE ☐
AID ☐

Test Paper 1

In the following questions, there are two pairs of words in brackets. Only one of the five answers will go equally well with both pairs. Select the correct word and mark it on the answer sheet.

1. (scratch scar) (sign symbol)
   spot dent mark badge stain

2. (criticise disapprove) (article gadget)
   device object dislike condemn itemise

3. (pebble boulder) (wobble totter)
   swing pitch rock stone crag

4. (gift show) (attendance current)
   award instant present donation register

5. (composition fragment) (portion selection)
   chunk share piece sample article

In the following questions, find the two words, one from each set of brackets, that are the most opposite in meaning. Mark the correct words on the answer sheet.

6. (volume whisper noise) (boom silence uproar)

7. (truth knowledge nonsense) (wisdom ignorance education)

8. (admiral leader command) (follower sailor order)

9. (work absent present) (holiday gift past)

10. (fake publicity fraud) (fame real dishonour)

In the following questions, one letter can be moved from the word on the left to the word on the right to form two new words. The letter may be removed from any position in the first word and placed in any position in the second word. No other letters may be rearranged. Mark the correct letter on the answer sheet.

11. TAPE SAT

12. WORLD HOW

13. BARE RING

14. DROWN OAR

15. NIECE LAP

In the following questions, find the letters that complete the sentence in the most sensible way. The alphabet is provided to help you. Mark the correct letters on the answer sheet.

A B C D E F G H I J K L M N O P Q R S T U V W X Y Z

16.   KM is to NP as RT is to _____

17.   GH is to EJ as NP is to _____

18.   PQ is to OP as DE is to _____

19.   KL is to PQ as TU is to _____

20.   AB is to XY as PR is to _____

In the following questions, find the number that continues the series in the most sensible way. Mark the correct number on the answer sheet.

21.   3   6   9   15   24   39   _____

22.   2   4   12   48   240   _____

23.   11   12   13   15   15   18   17   _____

24.   80   78   40   74   20   70   10   _____

25.   321   442   563   684   _____

In the following questions, there are three pairs of words. Find the word that completes the last pair of words in the same way as in the first two pairs. Mark the correct word on the answer sheet.

26.   GASP   PAGE   :   RASH   HARE   :   LOOP   _____

27.   DREAD   DARE   :   BLEAT   TALE   :   CREAM   _____

28.   LEANT   NEAT   :   BEATS   TEAS   :   PEARL   _____

29.   STRAW   ART   :   STARE   RAT   :   DWARF   _____

30.   LADDER   READ   :   CARPET   TEAR   :   RANDOM   _____

In the following questions, the same letter must fit in both sets of brackets to complete the word in front of the brackets and begin the word after the brackets. Mark the correct letter on the answer sheet.

31.   GUL ( ) EAR : PO ( ) AST

32.   CAS ( ) ATE : BOT ( ) EAR

33.　CO　( )　RIST　:　KNE　( )　ENT

34.　FAL　( )　OW　:　TEL　( )　AWN

35.　IN　( )　ITE　:　LUC　( )　ERB

In the following questions, there are two sets of words. The word in the brackets on the left hand side has been formed using some of the letters from the words on either side of the brackets. Form the missing word in the brackets on the right hand side from its pair of words, in the same way. Mark the newly formed word on the answer sheet.

36.　CARE　(STEP)　STOP　:　MEAN　( )　WARE

37.　LEND　(DEAF)　FLAT　:　NEAR　( )　TONE

38.　TIER　(HARE)　RASH　:　STEM　( )　BUST

39.　SWAP　(WAIT)　ITEM　:　DRAIN　( )　IDEA

40.　REAM　(MARE)　JUTE　:　CHAP　( )　PAST

In the following questions, one of the words from the bracket on the left can be joined to a word from the bracket on the right to form a completely new and proper word. Mark the two correct words on the answer sheet.

41.　(ALL　END　INK)　(LINE　TOGETHER　LESS)

42.　(HAND　ADD　CARE)　(FULL　FREE　SUN)

43.　(CARRY　NOTE　LESS)　(ABLE　ON　BAG)

44.　(CUP　SUN　TEAR)　(FULL　WEATHER　BOARD)

45.　(INN　NOT　BE)　(HIRE　VISIBLE　HAVE)

In the following questions, find the two words, one from each set of brackets, that will complete the sentence in the most sensible way. Mark the correct words on the answer sheet.

46.　Expel is to (leave, school, eject) as mend is to (patch, thoughtful, damage).

47.　Merciful is to (ruler, judge, cruel) as part is to (actor, play, whole).

48.　Dislike is to (enjoy, hate, favourite) as inspire is to (unite, encourage, lead).

49.　Centimetre is to (metre, measurement, distance) as year is to (month, century, time).

50.　Pair is to (fruit, gloves, two) as triple is to (jump, three, multiply).

In the following questions, three of the five words are related in some way. Which two words do not belong with the three related words? Mark the correct words on the answer sheet.

51.   run walk sprint crawl jog

52.   succeed precede achieve winner triumph

53.   pleasant lucky agreeable looking enchanting

54.   guess measure estimate weigh approximate

55.   slap pain strike punish whack

In the following sentences, a four-letter word can be formed from the letters at the end of one word and the beginning of the next, without changing the order of the letters. Find the hidden word and mark it on the answer sheet.

56.   The lion that escaped was soon captured.

57.   It is important that members of the choir sing.

58.   After the race each entrant was given an award.

59.   The penalty award made the players hopping mad.

60.   The presence of boys lowers the standard of behaviour.

In the following questions, find the letter or letters that continue(s) the series in the most sensible way. The alphabet is provided to help you. Mark the correct letter(s) on the answer sheet.

A B C D E F G H I J K L M N O P Q R S T U V W X Y Z

61.   E   F   H   K   O

62.   P   O   M   J   F

63.   JK   IL   HM   GN

64.   E   G   J   N   S

65.   B   F   D   H   F   J   H

In the following questions, a different code is used for each question. The first word has been worked out for you. Work out the second word, using the same code. The alphabet is provided to help you. Mark the correct word on the answer sheet.

A B C D E F G H I J K L M N O P Q R S T U V W X Y Z

66.   If the code word for COAT is EQCV what does UKPM represent?

67.   If the code word for TAXI is RCVK what does HWJA represent?

68.   If the code word for ROAST is TQCUV what is BREAD in the same code?

69.   If the code word for CAPE is EYRC what is the code for GOAL?

70.   If the code word for ROBE is UREH what is the code for CARE?

In the following questions, find the two words, one from each set of brackets, that are the closest in meaning. Mark the correct words on the answer sheet.

71.   (water   deluge   ice)   (multitude   flood   drizzle)

72.   (colossal   castle   size)   (defence   tower   massive)

73.   (music   silence   clamour)   (noise   opera   study)

74.   (police   honour   laws)   (parents   order   respect)

75.   (rebel   navy   sailors)   (mutiny   army   soldiers)

In each of the following sentences, the letters in capitals are missing three consecutive letters that can be inserted into the capital letters to form a word that completes the sentence. The three consecutive letters themselves form a sensible word. Mark the missing three-letter word on the answer sheet.

76.   Children should keep to the SHOW end of the pool.

77.   She MISK her for another person.

78.   He took his bucket and SE to the seaside.

79.   The headmaster GRED permission for his absence.

80.   The prisoner APLED for mercy.

Anthem Test Papers
11+ and 12+ Verbal Reasoning Book 1
Answer Sheet 2

Please select your answers by filling in the correct boxes.

Name:

1
- B ☐
- O ☐
- N ☐
- E ☐

2
- A ☐
- N ☐
- E ☐
- T ☐

3
- A ☐
- B ☐
- L ☐
- E ☐

4
- B ☐
- U ☐
- L ☐
- Y ☐

5
- T ☐
- O ☐
- S ☐
- E ☐

6
- 29 ☐
- 28 ☐
- 27 ☐
- 26 ☐
- 25 ☐

7
- 31 ☐
- 32 ☐
- 33 ☐
- 34 ☐
- 35 ☐

8
- 12 ☐
- 11 ☐
- 10 ☐
- 9 ☐
- 8 ☐

9
- 144 ☐
- 216 ☐
- 360 ☐
- 720 ☐
- 1008 ☐

10
- 19 ☐
- 20 ☐
- 21 ☐
- 22 ☐
- 23 ☐

11
- CROW ☐
- CREW ☐
- FLOW ☐
- ROLE ☐
- FLEW ☐

12
- BENT ☐
- TONE ☐
- NEON ☐
- BEEN ☐
- TEXT ☐

13
- LATE ☐
- REAL ☐
- TALE ☐
- TEAR ☐
- TAPE ☐

14
- TEST ☐
- PEST ☐
- PEER ☐
- TREE ☐
- SEEP ☐

15
- LOST ☐
- SOAP ☐
- STOP ☐
- POST ☐
- PAST ☐

16
- border ☐
- area ☐
- interior ☐
- edge ☐
- perimeter ☐

17
- courage ☐
- valour ☐
- timidity ☐
- cowardice ☐
- heroism ☐

18
- demolish ☐
- raze ☐
- construct ☐
- erect ☐
- build ☐

19
- remote ☐
- public ☐
- open ☐
- isolated ☐
- secluded ☐

20
- dwindle ☐
- intensity ☐
- heighten ☐
- subside ☐
- decrease ☐

21
- SNVMD ☐
- SNVNE ☐
- SNUME ☐
- SNVME ☐
- SNWME ☐

22
- SPEAR ☐
- SPEAK ☐
- SPADE ☐
- SPEED ☐
- SPARE ☐

23
- CQDX ☐
- CQDY ☐
- DQDY ☐
- CRDX ☐
- BQDX ☐

24
- CARD ☐
- CARE ☐
- CARS ☐
- CART ☐
- CARP ☐

25
- YXYX ☐
- ZXZY ☐
- ZAYX ☐
- ZYYX ☐
- ZYXX ☐

26
- NP ☐
- MP ☐
- NM ☐
- NQ ☐
- NO ☐

27
- TV ☐
- VV ☐
- SV ☐
- SW ☐
- SU ☐

28
- UZ ☐
- VZ ☐
- TY ☐
- TZ ☐
- VW ☐

29
- TQ ☐
- TR ☐
- SQ ☐
- SP ☐
- SW ☐

30
- OY ☐
- OX ☐
- OZ ☐
- PZ ☐
- QZ ☐

31
- 29 ☐
- 37 ☐
- 13 ☐
- 50 ☐
- 5 ☐

32
- 72 ☐
- 78 ☐
- 9 ☐
- 8 ☐
- 7 ☐

33
- 3 ☐
- 48 ☐
- 66 ☐
- 16 ☐
- 40 ☐

34
- 3 ☐
- 64 ☐
- 40 ☐
- 16 ☐
- 80 ☐

35
- 90 ☐
- 78 ☐
- 53 ☐
- 21 ☐
- 45 ☐

36
- U ☐
- V ☐
- W ☐
- X ☐
- Y ☐

37
- G ☐
- H ☐
- I ☐
- J ☐
- K ☐

38
- F ☐
- K ☐
- H ☐
- M ☐
- O ☐

39
- K ☐
- L ☐
- M ☐
- H ☐
- N ☐

40
- J ☐
- K ☐
- L ☐
- M ☐
- N ☐

Answer Sheet 2

Please select your answers by
filling in the correct boxes.

41
- CASES ☐
- EASES ☐
- RACES ☐
- SCARE ☐
- CARES ☐

42
- CASES ☐
- EASES ☐
- RACES ☐
- SCARE ☐
- CARES ☐

43
- CASES ☐
- EASES ☐
- RACES ☐
- SCARE ☐
- CARES ☐

44
- CASES ☐
- EASES ☐
- RACES ☐
- SCARE ☐
- CARES ☐

45
- CASES ☐
- EASES ☐
- RACES ☐
- SCARE ☐
- CARES ☐

46

HELL	☐	MET	☐
PLAT	☐	FORM	☐
FULL	☐	FILL	☐

47

TRAFFIC	☐	LIGHT	☐
SEA	☐	GULL	☐
PELICAN	☐	CROSSING	☐

48

HAVE	☐	BE	☐
TON	☐	AGE	☐
CAN	☐	NOT	☐

49

SEA	☐	GIN	☐
SIDE	☐	HIVE	☐
BE	☐	LEAVE	☐

50

CAP	☐	SIDE	☐
NO	☐	ICE	☐
FROZEN	☐	SIZE	☐

51
- B ☐
- Y ☐
- D ☐
- P ☐
- N ☐

52
- D ☐
- T ☐
- S ☐
- B ☐
- G ☐

53
- T ☐
- P ☐
- W ☐
- L ☐
- D ☐

54
- D ☐
- G ☐
- F ☐
- T ☐
- N ☐

55
- S ☐
- B ☐
- C ☐
- E ☐
- F ☐

56
- Alas the ☐
- the summer ☐
- is coming ☐
- to an ☐
- an end ☐

57
- Write your ☐
- your name ☐
- name and ☐
- and address ☐
- address here ☐

58
- He left ☐
- left his ☐
- his umbrella ☐
- umbrella on ☐
- the train ☐

59
- Bottles and ☐
- and paper ☐
- paper littered ☐
- littered the ☐
- the ground ☐

60
- He discovers ☐
- discovers old ☐
- old coins ☐
- coins for ☐
- a hobby ☐

61

cabbage	☐	fish	☐
robin	☐	vegetable	☐
sheep	☐	insect	☐

62

calf	☐	horse	☐
puppy	☐	lion	☐
lamb	☐	dog	☐

63

rung	☐	ladder	☐
wood	☐	climb	☐
rail	☐	slope	☐

64

weep	☐	old	☐
frown	☐	ill	☐
laugh	☐	cross	☐

65

door	☐	road	☐
smoke	☐	ship	☐
funnel	☐	cottage	☐

66

robust	☐	open	☐
weak	☐	strong	☐
great	☐	red	☐

67

rough	☐	aid	☐
help	☐	calm	☐
small	☐	stop	☐

68

down	☐	moon	☐
bright	☐	shining	☐
sun	☐	up	☐

69

peculiar	☐	take	☐
join	☐	give	☐
gain	☐	strange	☐

70

feeble	☐	weak	☐
strong	☐	tiger	☐
lion	☐	iron	☐

71
- T ☐
- U ☐
- V ☐
- W ☐
- X ☐

72
- T ☐
- U ☐
- V ☐
- W ☐
- X ☐

73
- T ☐
- U ☐
- V ☐
- W ☐
- X ☐

74
- T ☐
- U ☐
- V ☐
- W ☐
- X ☐

75
- T ☐
- U ☐
- V ☐
- W ☐
- X ☐

76
- ARE ☐
- AND ☐
- OUR ☐
- OUT ☐
- NOR ☐

77
- SAT ☐
- SAD ☐
- SIT ☐
- OLD ☐
- LAP ☐

78
- AND ☐
- END ☐
- FLY ☐
- DID ☐
- MET ☐

79
- LAY ☐
- AND ☐
- SAD ☐
- DID ☐
- BID ☐

80
- BID ☐
- SAD ☐
- TEA ☐
- SAT ☐
- ATE ☐

Test Paper 2

In the following questions, one letter can be moved from the word on the left to the word on the right to form two new words. The letter may be removed from any position in the first word and placed in any position in the second word. No other letters may be rearranged. Mark the correct letter on the answer sheet.

1.   BONE   LESS

2.   PLANET   STEP

3.   TABLE   LOW

4.   BULLY   EAR

5.   THOSE   CAR

In the following questions, find the number that continues the series in the most sensible way. Mark the correct number on the answer sheet.

6.   47   45   42   38   33   _____

7.   17   20   21   22   25   24   29   26   _____

8.   19   18   17   16   15   14   13   _____

9.   3   3   6   18   72   _____

10. 2   3   5   8   13   _____

In the following questions, there are two sets of words. The word in the brackets on the left hand side has been formed using some of the letters from the words on either side of the brackets. Form the missing word in the brackets on the right hand side from its pair of words, in the same way. Mark the newly formed word on the answer sheet.

11. FLOW   (FLAG)   SNAG   :   CROW   (   )   FLEW

12. SOAP   (SPAN)   NAPE   :   BONE   (   )   NEXT

13. WALL   (LATE)   MEET   :   RATE   (   )   PEEL

14. CLAP   (PAIN)   NICE   :   STEP   (   )   REST

15. CAST   (SAFE)   CAFE   :   MOST   (   )   SLAP

In the following questions, three of the five words are related in some way. Which two words do not belong with the three related words? Mark the correct words on the answer sheet.

16.   border   area   interior   edge   perimeter

17.   courage   valour   timidity   cowardice   heroism

18.   demolish   raze   construct   erect   build

19.   remote   public   open   isolated   secluded

20.   dwindle   intensity   heighten   subside   decrease

In the following questions, a different code is used for each question. The first word has been worked out for you. Work out the second word, using the same code. The alphabet is provided to help you. Mark the correct word on the answer sheet.

A B C D E F G H I J K L M N O P Q R S T U V W X Y Z

21.   If the code word for PEARS is QDBQT what is the code for ROUND?

22.   If the code word for PRIDE is OSHED what does RQDFC represent?

23.   If the code word for SOAP is TQDT what is BOAT in the same code?

24.   If the code word for PLAN is OJXJ what does BYOP represent?

25.   If the code word for ROPE is XYZQ what is the code for POOR?

In the following questions, find the letters that complete the sentence in the most sensible way. The alphabet is provided to help you. Mark the correct letters on the answer sheet.

A B C D E F G H I J K L M N O P Q R S T U V W X Y Z

26.   DE is to FG as LM is to _____

27.   KM is to JN as TU is to _____

28.   PQ is to NS as WX is to _____

29.   KL is to KI as ST is to _____

30.   BG is to XK as SV is to _____

In the following questions, the three numbers in each group are related in the same way. Find the number that completes the last group. Mark the correct number on the answer sheet.

31.   5 (6) 11   7 (12) 19   8 ( ) 21

32.   39 (3) 13   48 (8) 6   84 ( ) 12

33.   17 (70) 18   37 (122) 24   18 ( ) 15

34.   68 (52) 18   76 (62) 24   48 ( ) 16

35.   17 (30) 43   37 (25) 13   16 ( ) 74

In each of the following questions, find the letter that continues the series in the most sensible way. The alphabet is provided to help you. Mark the correct letter on the answer sheet.

A B C D E F G H I J K L M N O P Q R S T U V W X Y Z

36.   C   E   H   L   Q   _____

37.   W   V   T   Q   M   _____

38.   C   D   E   F   G   _____

39.   M   N   O   L   Q   J   S   _____

40.   M   N   L   M   K   L   J   _____

In the following questions, the words CASES, EASES, RACES, SCARE, and CARES have been coded into symbols. Match each set of symbols with its corresponding word. Mark the correct word on the answer sheet.

41.   ? 0 + ! X

42.   X + 0 ? !

43.   + 0 X ! X

44.   ! 0 X ! X

45.   + 0 ? ! X

In the following questions, one of the words from the bracket on the left can be joined to a word from the bracket on the right to form a completely new and proper word. Mark the two correct words on the answer sheet.

46.   (HELL PLAT FULL)   (MET FORM FILL)

47.   (TRAFFIC SEA PELICAN)   (LIGHT GULL CROSSING)

48.   (HAVE TON CAN)   (BE AGE NOT)

49.   (SEA SIDE BE)   (GIN HIVE LEAVE)

50.   (CAP NO FROZEN)   (SIDE ICE SIZE)

In the following questions, the same letter must fit in both sets of brackets to complete the word in front of the brackets and begin the word after the brackets. Mark the correct letter on the answer sheet.

51.   VER ( ) ACHT   SA ( ) EAR

52.   WRIN ( ) RAIN   SIN ( ) LOW

53.   CRIS ( ) RICE   SEE ( ) AIR

54.   BEN ( ) EAR   SIGH ( ) ORE

55.   ROB ( ) ACH   BAR ( ) AT

In the following sentences, a four-letter word can be formed from the letters at the end of one word and the beginning of the next, without changing the order of the letters. Find the hidden word and mark it on the answer sheet.

56.   Alas the summer is coming to an end.

57.   Write your name and address here.

58.   He left his umbrella on the train.

59.   Bottles and paper littered the ground.

60.   He discovers old coins for a hobby.

In the following questions, find the two words, one from each set of brackets, that will complete the sentence in the most sensible way. Mark the correct words on the answer sheet.

61.   Apple is to fruit as (cabbage, robin, sheep) is to (fish, vegetable, insect).

62.   Kitten is to cat as (calf, puppy, lamb) is to (horse, lion, dog).

63. Step is to stair as (rung, wood, rail) is to (ladder, climb, slope).

64. Smile is to pleased as (weep, frown, laugh) is to (old, ill, cross).

65. Chimney is to house as (door, smoke, funnel) is to (road, ship, cottage).

In the following questions, find the two words, one from each set of brackets, that are the closest in meaning. Mark the correct words on the answer sheet.

66. (robust weak great)   (open strong red)

67. (rough help small)   (aid calm stop)

68. (down bright sun)   (moon shining up)

69. (peculiar join gain)   (take give strange)

70. (feeble strong lion)   (weak tiger iron)

In the following questions, $T = 8$, $U = 4$, $V = 5$, $W = 2$ and $X = 3$. Work out the values of the following, giving your answer as a letter. Mark the correct letter on the answer sheet.

71. $\dfrac{T}{W}$

72. $T - (X + W)$

73. $\dfrac{(V + T) - X}{W}$

74. $\dfrac{WT}{T}$

75. $\dfrac{UWX}{T}$

In each of the following sentences, the letters in capitals are missing three consecutive letters that can be inserted into the capital letters to form a word that completes the sentence. The three consecutive letters themselves form a sensible word. Mark the missing three-letter word on the answer sheet.

76. The painting had many brilliant COLS.

77. The deckchair COLSED under the man's weight.

78. The balloon ASCED.

79. The bus was DEED in the traffic.

80. The champion was DEFED by the challenger.

Anthem Test Papers
11+ and 12+ Verbal Reasoning Book 1
Answer Sheet 3

Please select your answers by
filling in the correct boxes.

Name:

1
RATE ☐
TALE ☐
TEAR ☐
TARE ☐
REAL ☐

2
DINE ☐
NINE ☐
RIND ☐
RIDE ☐
REIN ☐

3
KITE ☐
KICK ☐
KNEE ☐
KILT ☐
KIND ☐

4
SAY ☐
SKI ☐
SLY ☐
SKY ☐
SAT ☐

5
RAINS ☐
RAILS ☐
RAISE ☐
RALLY ☐
RATES ☐

6
S ☐
T ☐
U ☐
W ☐
T ☐

7
X ☐
T ☐
W ☐
U ☐
V ☐

8
G ☐
F ☐
E ☐
D ☐
C ☐

9
M ☐
V ☐
W ☐
X ☐
L ☐

10
MU ☐
LU ☐
KX ☐
KV ☐
KU ☐

11
25 ☐
26 ☐
27 ☐
28 ☐
29 ☐

12
1200 ☐
2400 ☐
3600 ☐
7200 ☐
9500 ☐

13
102 ☐
98 ☐
96 ☐
100 ☐
104 ☐

14
12 ☐
15 ☐
13 ☐
11 ☐
17 ☐

15
40 ☐
54 ☐
64 ☐
51 ☐
44 ☐

16
ACRE ☐
RACE ☐
RARE ☐
REAR ☐
CARE ☐

17
ACRE ☐
RACE ☐
RARE ☐
REAR ☐
CARE ☐

18
ACRE ☐
RACE ☐
RARE ☐
REAR ☐
CARE ☐

19
ACRE ☐
RACE ☐
RARE ☐
REAR ☐
CARE ☐

20
9.10am ☐
9.12am ☐
9.15am ☐
9.21am ☐
9.30am ☐

21
L ☐
A ☐
T ☐
H ☐
E ☐

22
F ☐
I ☐
O ☐
R ☐
D ☐

23
R ☐
I ☐
N ☐
S ☐
E ☐

24
L ☐
A ☐
N ☐
C ☐
E ☐

25
M ☐
A ☐
I ☐
Z ☐
E ☐

26
Bill ☐
Fred ☐
Harry ☐
Ann ☐
Pat ☐

27
Bill ☐
Fred ☐
Harry ☐
Ann ☐
Pat ☐

28
plane ☐
car ☐
train ☐
sea ☐

29
1 ☐
2 ☐
3 ☐
4 ☐

30
Bill ☐
Fred ☐
Harry ☐
Ann ☐
Pat ☐

31
T ☐
E ☐
Y ☐
K ☐
H ☐

32
E ☐
D ☐
Y ☐
T ☐
N ☐

33
G ☐
Y ☐
B ☐
R ☐
C ☐

34
Y ☐
W ☐
P ☐
F ☐
D ☐

35
T ☐
N ☐
B ☐
W ☐
H ☐

36
pork ☐ grass ☐
sow ☐ milk ☐
piglet ☐ beef ☐

37
ring ☐ foot ☐
hand ☐ bone ☐
point ☐ wrist ☐

38
whisper ☐ shoe ☐
loud ☐ track ☐
voice ☐ walk ☐

39
bird ☐ fruit ☐
shell ☐ juice ☐
crack ☐ rind ☐

40
hot ☐ fool ☐
July ☐ showers ☐
tennis ☐ May ☐

Answer Sheet 3

Please select your answers by
filling in the correct boxes.

41
- CAT ☐
- SAT ☐
- HAS ☐
- HAT ☐

42
- TAN ☐
- SAT ☐
- CAN ☐
- CAT ☐

43
- STAB ☐
- SITS ☐
- BATS ☐
- BEST ☐

44
- TONE ☐
- BONE ☐
- DONE ☐
- HONE ☐

45
- SAT ☐
- TAB ☐
- BET ☐
- BAT ☐

46
- CAN ☐
- BAN ☐
- SIN ☐
- ONE ☐

47
- ARE ☐
- SIN ☐
- OUR ☐
- PIN ☐

48
- ICE ☐
- CAN ☐
- TEN ☐
- TIN ☐

49
- RUN ☐
- CAR ☐
- RAT ☐
- DIN ☐

50
- OUT ☐
- CAP ☐
- CAT ☐
- PIT ☐

51
- Add Two ☐
- two odd ☐
- odd numbers ☐
- the answer ☐
- be even ☐

52
- A popular ☐
- popular favourite ☐
- favourite story ☐
- story is ☐
- is Cinderella ☐

53
- There are ☐
- three school ☐
- school terms ☐
- terms each ☐
- each year ☐

54
- The ape ☐
- ape roared ☐
- roared at ☐
- at the ☐
- the visitors ☐

55
- Time and ☐
- and again ☐
- again the ☐
- the pupils ☐
- pupils misbehaved ☐

56
- This ☐
- selected ☐
- Harry ☐
- will ☐
- time ☐

57
- sailed ☐
- ship ☐
- the ☐
- silently ☐
- port ☐

58
- boys ☐
- number ☐
- coats ☐
- peg ☐
- hung ☐

59
- Cars ☐
- park ☐
- were ☐
- busy ☐
- street ☐

60
- Broke ☐
- the ☐
- storm ☐
- clouds ☐
- after ☐

61
- drive ☐
- power ☐
- force ☐
- command ☐
- impact ☐

62
- taken ☐
- feature ☐
- mark ☐
- blot ☐
- symbol ☐

63
- piece ☐
- division ☐
- section ☐
- part ☐
- divide ☐

64
- journal ☐
- report ☐
- record ☐
- inscribe ☐
- documents ☐

65
- gap ☐
- opening ☐
- break ☐
- crevice ☐
- collapse ☐

66
- 70 ☐
- 55 ☐
- 110 ☐
- 60 ☐
- 65 ☐

67
- 20 ☐
- 40 ☐
- 75 ☐
- 100 ☐
- 125 ☐

68
- 24 ☐
- 28 ☐
- 18 ☐
- 69 ☐
- 12 ☐

69
- 64 ☐
- 45 ☐
- 18 ☐
- 30 ☐
- 15 ☐

70
- 8 ☐
- 24 ☐
- 40 ☐
- 48 ☐
- 64 ☐

71
- trumpet ☐
- piano ☐
- violin ☐
- saxophone ☐
- bugle ☐

72
- helmet ☐
- cap ☐
- beret ☐
- head ☐
- hair ☐

73
- hammer ☐
- carpenter ☐
- saw ☐
- nail ☐
- screwdriver ☐

74
- leave ☐
- enter ☐
- abandon ☐
- vacate ☐
- occupy ☐

75
- expose ☐
- part ☐
- reveal ☐
- keep ☐
- show ☐

76
- X ☐
- Y ☐
- B ☐
- P ☐
- Q ☐

77
- X ☐
- Y ☐
- B ☐
- P ☐
- Q ☐

78
- X ☐
- Y ☐
- B ☐
- P ☐
- Q ☐

79
- X ☐
- Y ☐
- B ☐
- P ☐
- Q ☐

80
- X ☐
- Y ☐
- B ☐
- P ☐
- Q ☐

Test Paper 3

In the following questions, a different code is used for each question. The first word has been worked out for you. Work out the second word, using the same code. The alphabet is provided to help you. Mark the correct word on the answer sheet.

A B C D E F G H I J K L M N O P Q R S T U V W X Y Z

1. If DUVNQU stands for RELATE then what does QNVU represent?

2. If CRTTVP stands for DINNER then what does PRTC represent?

3. If APSCJ stands for CRUEL then what does IGLB represent?

4. If HQPTOC stands for GROUND then what does TJZ represent?

5. If XPTQVW stands for SAILOR then what does WPTQX represent?

In the following questions, find the letter or letters that continue(s) the series in the most sensible way. The alphabet is provided to help you. Mark the correct letter(s) on the answer sheet.

A B C D E F G H I J K L M N O P Q R S T U V W X Y Z

6. A C F J O _____

7. A G L P S _____

8. Z T O K H _____

9. A Z D Y G X J _____

10. AZ CY EX GW IV _____

In the following questions, find the number that continues the series in the most sensible way. Mark the correct number on the answer sheet.

11. 7 11 15 19 23 _____

12. 5 10 30 120 600 _____

13. 140 132 124 116 108 _____

14. 3 5 6 8 9 _____

15. 3 7 10 17 27 _____

In the following questions, the words ACRE, RACE, RARE, REAR, and CARE have been coded into symbols. Match each set of symbols with its corresponding word. Mark the correct word on the answer sheet.

16.   ◊ + □ ◊

17.   ◊ □ ? +

18.   ◊ □ ◊ +

19.   □ ? ◊ +

20.   Tom had an appointment in London at 11.45am. The train journey usually lasts 2 hours 15 minutes but, on this occasion, the train was 12 minutes late. What time did the train depart if he arrived with three minutes to spare? Mark the correct time on the answer sheet.

In the following questions, one letter can be moved from the word on the left to the word on the right to form two new words. The letter may be removed from any position in the first word and placed in any position in the second word. No other letters may be rearranged. Mark the correct letter on the answer sheet.

21.   LATHER   AND

22.   FIORD   BAT

23.   RINSE   KIT

24.   LANCE   HARM

25.   MAIZE   NOSE

Bill, Fred, Harry, Ann and Pat were asked whether they had travelled on their holidays by plane, car, train or sea. Each could have used any or all forms of transportation. Bill and Harry had travelled by plane. Fred and Pat had travelled by car. Only Fred and Harry had not travelled by train. Bill, Harry and Ann had not travelled by sea. For the following questions, mark the correct person on the answer sheet.

26.   Who had travelled by just plane and train?

27.   Who had travelled by just car and sea?

28.   What was the most used form of travel?

29.   How many methods of travel had been used by Harry?

30.   Who used three forms of travel?

In the following questions, the same letter must fit in both sets of brackets to complete the word in front of the brackets and begin the word after the brackets. Mark the correct letter on the answer sheet.

31.   CAS ( ) ARN   LAC ( ) VIL

32.   BOR ( ) EAR   LEA ( ) EXT

33.   STA ( ) LOT   CLU ( ) RICK

34.   STRA ( ) ORT   LEA ( ) RAY

35.   SLO ( ) OOD   PE ( ) ASH

In the following questions, find the two words, one from each set of brackets, that will complete the sentence in the most sensible way. Mark the correct words on the answer sheet.

36.   Pig is to (pork, sow, piglet) as cow is to (grass, milk, beef).

37.   Finger is to (ring, hand, point) as toe is to (foot, bone, wrist).

38.   Shout is to (whisper, loud, voice) as run is to (shoe, track, walk).

39.   Egg is to (bird, shell, crack) as orange is to (fruit, juice, rind).

40.   June is to (hot, July, tennis) as April is to (fool, showers, May).

In the following questions, there are three pairs of words. Find the word that completes the last pair of words in the same way as in the first two pairs. Mark the correct word on the answer sheet.

41.   SHAME   HAM   :   SCARE   CAR   :   CHATS _____

42.   STAIN   TAN   :   TRAIN   RAN   :   SCANT _____

43.   MACE   CAME :   MATE   TAME   :   TABS   _____

44.   BARE   CARE :   SOOT   TOOT   :   CONE   _____

45.   STUNT   NUT   :   STORE   ROT   :   STABS _____

In each of the following sentences, the letters in capitals are missing three consecutive letters that can be inserted into the capital letters to form a word that completes the sentence. The three consecutive letters themselves form a sensible word. Mark the missing three-letter word on the answer sheet.

46.   Millionaires have lots of MY to spend on presents.

47.   All TISTS in London like to see Big Ben.

48.   The lazy pupil was OF off school.

49.   London MAHON is every year in late spring.

50.   The fielder dropped a straightforward CH.

In the following sentences, a four-letter word can be formed from the letters at the end of one word and the beginning of the next, without changing the order of the letters. Find the hidden word and mark it on the answer sheet.

51.   Add two odd numbers then the answer will be even.

52.   A popular favourite story is Cinderella.

53.   There are three school terms each year.

54.   The ape roared at the visitors.

55.   Time and again the pupils misbehaved.

In each of the following sentences, two words must exchange places for the sentence to make sense. Mark the two correct words on the answer sheet.

56.   This selected Harry will be time.

57.   Sailed ship the silently into port.

58.   Two boys number their coats on peg hung ten.

59.   Cars park unable to were in the busy street.

60.   Broke the storm the clouds after up.

In the following questions, two pairs of words are given in brackets. Only one of the five answers will go equally well with both pairs. Mark the correct word on the answer sheet.

61.   (compel order)   (aggression violence)
       drive power force command impact

62.   (correct assess)   (scar scratch)
       taken feature mark blot symbol

63.   (fraction portion)   (split separate)
       piece division section part divide

64.   (tape unbeaten)   (file diary)
       journal report record inscribe documents

65.   (destroy split)   (shatter rest)
       gap opening break crevice collapse

In the following questions, the three numbers in each group are related in the same way. Find the number that completes the last group. Mark the correct number on the answer sheet.

66.   60 (50) 20   70 (43) 8   90 ( ) 20

67.   6 (42) 7   4 (36) 9   5 ( ) 15

68.   17 (10) 13   41 (20) 19   39 ( ) 15

69.   23 (5) 2   17 (8) 23   13 ( ) 77

70.   7 (29) 11   11 (21) 5   8 ( ) 16

In the following questions, three of the five words are related in some way. Which two words do not belong with the three related words? Mark the correct words on the answer sheet.

71.   trumpet piano violin saxophone bugle

72.   helmet cap beret head hair

73.   hammer carpenter saw nail screwdriver

74.   leave enter abandon vacate occupy

75.   expose part reveal keep show

In the following questions, X = 6, Y = 2, B = 4, P = 5 and Q = 1. Work out the values of the following, giving your answer as a letter. Mark the correct letter on the answer sheet.

76. $Y + P - Q$

77. $X - P + Q$

78. $X + Y - P + Y$

79. $\dfrac{X + Q}{Y}$

80. $P + Q - B$

Anthem Test Papers
11+ and 12+ Verbal Reasoning Book 1
Answer Sheet 4

Please select your answers by filling in the correct boxes.

Name:

1
CRACK	☐	FAST	☐
BREAK	☐	SPEED	☐
STRIKE	☐	RATE	☐

2
CAR	☐	TIN	☐
BUS	☐	PET	☐
TRAM	☐	CAT	☐

3
TEE	☐	OBJECT	☐
NO	☐	POT	☐
DRESS	☐	THING	☐

4
PLAY	☐	OR	☐
ACT	☐	BY	☐
SCENE	☐	TO	☐

5
DESK	☐	SILK	☐
TABLE	☐	CLOTH	☐
STOOL	☐	FELT	☐

6
LENDER	☐
TENDER	☐
KINDER	☐
SENDER	☐

7
HOSE	☐
HOPE	☐
EACH	☐
ECHO	☐

8
TEAS	☐
DATE	☐
EASE	☐
SEAT	☐

9
WEED	☐
SEED	☐
DEED	☐
FEED	☐

10
MEAL	☐
MAIL	☐
MALT	☐
MALE	☐

11
PLOT	☐
PLUG	☐
PLUM	☐
PLEA	☐
PLUS	☐

12
SCORE	☐
SCONE	☐
SCOPE	☐
SCOUR	☐
SCOWL	☐

13
PAIR	☐
PAIL	☐
PAID	☐
PALM	☐
PAIN	☐

14
SCAMP	☐
SCORN	☐
SCORE	☐
SCOUT	☐
SCRAP	☐

15
FILE	☐
FILL	☐
FLAG	☐
FIRE	☐
FIVE	☐

16
16	☐
12	☐
8	☐
4	☐
3	☐

17
16	☐
24	☐
32	☐
48	☐
64	☐

18
3	☐
13	☐
11	☐
21	☐
40	☐

19
14	☐
22	☐
23	☐
28	☐
33	☐

20
16	☐
22	☐
44	☐
60	☐
70	☐

21
Many rare	☐
rare stamps	☐
stamps are	☐
are often	☐
often unrecognised	☐

22
The air	☐
air high	☐
the mountains	☐
is always	☐
always refreshing	☐

23
Apple pie	☐
pie remains	☐
remains a	☐
a popular	☐
popular pudding	☐

24
The extremely	☐
extremely valuable	☐
valuable missing	☐
missing ring	☐
was lost	☐

25
Always control	☐
control your	☐
your anger	☐
is sound	☐
sound advice	☐

26
rare	☐	valuable	☐
beautiful	☐	unusual	☐
antique	☐	expensive	☐

27
forgive	☐	penance	☐
apology	☐	pardon	☐
amend	☐	acquit	☐

28
quarter	☐	fraction	☐
part	☐	second	☐
third	☐	tenth	☐

29
cherish	☐	enjoy	☐
help	☐	love	☐
hate	☐	keep	☐

30
cloudy	☐	rainy	☐
foggy	☐	clear	☐
sunny	☐	misty	☐

31
theatre	☐	sermon	☐
audience	☐	prayer	☐
stage	☐	congregation	☐

32
pupil	☐	knowledge	☐
teacher	☐	reply	☐
doubt	☐	ignorance	☐

33
delight	☐	joy	☐
success	☐	victory	☐
sorrow	☐	failure	☐

Answer Sheet 4

Please select your answers by
filling in the correct boxes.

34
enormous ☐	minute ☐
fragile ☐	small ☐
weak ☐	huge ☐

35
noise ☐	glasses ☐
radio ☐	television ☐
hearing ☐	distance ☐

36
| NOT ☐ |
| SIT ☐ |
| NIT ☐ |
| PAT ☐ |
| PIN ☐ |

37
| OUT ☐ |
| TOO ☐ |
| SIN ☐ |
| OUR ☐ |
| FOR ☐ |

38
| APE ☐ |
| PEA ☐ |
| ATE ☐ |
| EAT ☐ |
| PAN ☐ |

39
| PER ☐ |
| PAR ☐ |
| PIP ☐ |
| SIP ☐ |
| CAN ☐ |

40
| LET ☐ |
| NEW ☐ |
| BED ☐ |
| NOW ☐ |
| SOW ☐ |

41
| C ☐ |
| A ☐ |
| R ☐ |
| E ☐ |

42
| F ☐ |
| L ☐ |
| O ☐ |
| W ☐ |
| E |

43
| P ☐ |
| R ☐ |
| I ☐ |
| D ☐ |
| E ☐ |

44
| S ☐ |
| C ☐ |
| A ☐ |
| L ☐ |
| E ☐ |

45
| W ☐ |
| I ☐ |
| N ☐ |
| D ☐ |
| O ☐ |

46
| 17 ☐ |
| 13 ☐ |
| 12 ☐ |
| 11 ☐ |
| 10 ☐ |

47
| 21 ☐ |
| 22 ☐ |
| 23 ☐ |
| 24 ☐ |
| 25 ☐ |

48
| 13 ☐ |
| 14 ☐ |
| 15 ☐ |
| 16 ☐ |
| 17 ☐ |

49
| 30 ☐ |
| 62 ☐ |
| 63 ☐ |
| 67 ☐ |
| 69 ☐ |

50
| 65 ☐ |
| 60 ☐ |
| 75 ☐ |
| 80 ☐ |
| 85 ☐ |

51
| WY ☐ |
| WX ☐ |
| XY ☐ |
| XV ☐ |
| XW ☐ |

52
| SU ☐ |
| TU ☐ |
| VT ☐ |
| VW ☐ |
| VU ☐ |

53
| NK ☐ |
| MK ☐ |
| LK ☐ |
| LL ☐ |
| LN ☐ |

54
| XU ☐ |
| XT ☐ |
| XV ☐ |
| YT ☐ |
| ZT ☐ |

55
| RSU ☐ |
| QTU ☐ |
| QSU ☐ |
| QSV ☐ |
| QST ☐ |

56
| A ☐ |
| B ☐ |
| C ☐ |
| D ☐ |
| E ☐ |

57
| A ☐ |
| B ☐ |
| C ☐ |
| D ☐ |
| E ☐ |

58
| A ☐ |
| B ☐ |
| C ☐ |
| D ☐ |
| E ☐ |

59
| A ☐ |
| B ☐ |
| C ☐ |
| D ☐ |
| E ☐ |

60
| A ☐ |
| B ☐ |
| C ☐ |
| D ☐ |
| E ☐ |

61
| Bill ☐ |
| John ☐ |
| Peter ☐ |
| Ann ☐ |
| Joan ☐ |

62
| Bill ☐ |
| John ☐ |
| Peter ☐ |
| Ann ☐ |
| Joan ☐ |

63
| Bill ☐ |
| John ☐ |
| Peter ☐ |
| Ann ☐ |
| Joan ☐ |

64
| Bill ☐ |
| John ☐ |
| Peter ☐ |
| Ann ☐ |
| Joan ☐ |

65
| Bill ☐ |
| John ☐ |
| Peter ☐ |
| Ann ☐ |
| Joan ☐ |

66
| jam ☐ |
| traverse ☐ |
| cross ☐ |
| annoyance ☐ |
| tempered ☐ |

67
| moat ☐ |
| discard ☐ |
| excavation ☐ |
| ditch ☐ |
| pit ☐ |

68
| accommodation ☐ |
| box ☐ |
| carton ☐ |
| blow ☐ |
| smack ☐ |

69
| pressure ☐ |
| prestige ☐ |
| power ☐ |
| position ☐ |
| skill ☐ |

70
| smooth ☐ |
| fashionable ☐ |
| neat ☐ |
| smart ☐ |
| sharp ☐ |

71
| JM ☐ |
| JL ☐ |
| JK ☐ |
| IK ☐ |
| GK ☐ |

72
| PN ☐ |
| MN ☐ |
| LI ☐ |
| LM ☐ |
| LO ☐ |

73
| LS ☐ |
| MS ☐ |
| NS ☐ |
| NT ☐ |
| NR ☐ |

74
| UR ☐ |
| UQ ☐ |
| UP ☐ |
| VQ ☐ |
| RQ ☐ |

75
| MG ☐ |
| NG ☐ |
| OG ☐ |
| OH ☐ |
| OF ☐ |

76
| alive ☐ |
| imagine ☐ |
| actual ☐ |
| impossible ☐ |
| thing ☐ |

77
| alter ☐ |
| enlarge ☐ |
| intend ☐ |
| extract ☐ |
| maintain ☐ |

78
| attack ☐ |
| sorrow ☐ |
| cruelty ☐ |
| hatred ☐ |
| wrath ☐ |

79
| agility ☐ |
| rush ☐ |
| enthusiasm ☐ |
| willingness ☐ |
| urge ☐ |

80
| inside ☐ |
| here ☐ |
| beyond ☐ |
| further ☐ |
| distant ☐ |

Test Paper 4

In the following questions, one of the words from the bracket on the left can be joined to a word from the bracket on the right to form a completely new and proper word. Mark the two correct words on the answer sheet.

1. (CRACK   BREAK   STRIKE)   (FAST   SPEED   RATE)

2. (CAR   BUS   TRAM)   (TIN   PET   CAT)

3. (TEE   NO   DRESS)   (OBJECT   POT   THING)

4. (PLAY   ACT   SCENE)   (OR   BY   TO)

5. (DESK   TABLE   STOOL)   (SILK   CLOTH   FELT)

In the following questions, there are three pairs of words. Find the word that completes the last pair of words in the same way as in the first two pairs. Mark the correct word on the answer sheet.

6. DEAL   LEADER : DINT   TINDER : DENS   _____

7. CARES   SCAR : ALLOW   WALL : CHOSE   _____

8. GRAVEL   RAGE : SPOKEN   POSE : SEATED   _____

9. SET   SEES : PEN   PEEP : DEW   _____

10. WHILE   MILE : WHOLE   MOLE : WHALE   _____

In the following questions, a different code is used for each question. The first word has been worked out for you. Work out the second word, using the same code. The alphabet is provided to help you. Mark the correct word on the answer sheet.

A B C D E F G H I J K L M N O P Q R S T U V W X Y Z

11. If SNBC stands for ROAD what does QKVL represent?

12. If QGDV stands for PEAR what does TERVJ represent?

13. If GSUP stands for BORN what does UELP represent?

14. If ITQCP stands for GROAN what does UEQTG represent?

15. If RDNSD stands for SCORE what does EJUF represent?

In the following questions, the three numbers in each group are related in the same way. Find the number that completes the last group. Mark the correct number on the answer sheet.

16.   18 (3) 6   15 (3) 5   24 ( ) 8

17.   8 (20) 5   6 (24) 8   8 ( ) 8

18.   9 (13) 5   7 (12) 2   8 ( ) 5

19.   12 (5) 8   28 (17) 40   32 ( ) 60

20.   15 (30) 4   21 (84) 8   12 ( ) 10

In the following questions, a four-letter word can be formed from the letters at the end of one word and the beginning of the next, without changing the order of the letters. Find the pair of words and mark it on the answer sheet.

21.   Many rare stamps are often unrecognised.

22.   The air high on the mountains is always refreshing.

23.   Apple pie remains a popular pudding.

24.   The extremely valuable missing ring was lost.

25.   Always control your anger is sound advice.

In the following questions, find the two words, one from each set of brackets, that are the closest in meaning. Mark the correct words on the answer sheet.

26.   (rare beautiful antique)   (valuable unusual expensive)

27.   (forgive apology amend)   (penance pardon acquit)

28.   (quarter part third)   (fraction second tenth)

29.   (cherish help hate)   (enjoy love keep)

30.   (cloudy foggy sunny)   (rainy clear misty)

In the following questions, find the two words, one from each set of brackets, that will complete the sentence in the most sensible way. Mark the correct words on the answer sheet.

31.   Actor is to (theatre, audience, stage) as preacher is to (sermon, prayer, congregation).

32.   Question is to (pupil, teacher, doubt) as answer is to (knowledge, reply, ignorance).

33. Happiness is to (delight, success, sorrow) as success is to (joy, victory, failure).

34. Tiny is to (enormous, fragile, weak) as microscopic is to (minute, small, huge).

35. Sound is to (noise, radio, hearing) as sight is to (glasses, television, distance).

In each of the following sentences, the letters in capitals are missing three consecutive letters that can be inserted into the capital letters to form a word that completes the sentence. The three consecutive letters themselves form a sensible word. Mark the missing three-letter word on the answer sheet.

36. In the OION of the referee it was a penalty.

37. The gentleman displayed great CTESY to the old lady.

38. The APRANCE of the headmaster made the pupils go silent.

39. It soon became APENT that the man was guilty.

40. The pupil displayed excellent KLEDGE in the examination.

In the following questions, one letter can be moved from the word on the left to the word on the right to form two new words. The letter may be removed from any position in the first word and placed in any position in the second word. No other letters may be rearranged. Mark the correct letter on the answer sheet.

41. CARE   POT

42. FLOWER   REED

43. PRIDE   SIN

44. SCALE   RAMP

45. WINDOW   KEEL

In the following questions, find the number that continues the series in the most sensible way. Mark the correct number on the answer sheet.

46.   20   21   18   19   16   17   14   15   _____

47.   2   4   5   10   11   22   _____

48.   3   4   6   8   9   12   12   16   _____

49.   0   1   3   7   15   31   _____

50.   0   10   21   33   46   60   _____

In the following questions, find the letters that complete the series in the most sensible way. The alphabet is provided to help you. Mark the correct letters on the answer sheet.

A B C D E F G H I J K L M N O P Q R S T U V W X Y Z

51.   KL   NO   QR   TU   _____

52.   NM   PO   RQ   TS   _____

53.   AB   DC   EF   HG   IJ   _____

54.   DB   FD   IG   MK   RP   _____

55.   BDF   EGI   HJL   KMO   NPR   _____

In the following questions, A = 5, B = 6, C = 11, D = 20, and E = 10. Work out the values of the following, giving your answer as a letter. Mark the correct letter on the answer sheet.

56. $C - B$

57. $B - C + 5A$

58. $A \times B - D$

59. $D + C - B - A - E$

60. $\dfrac{D + E}{B}$

Bill, John, Peter, Ann and Joan were asked which countries they had visited. Bill and John had visited the USA. John and Ann had visited France. Peter and Joan had visited Spain. Only John and Peter had not visited Germany. Peter was the only visitor to Portugal. For the following questions, mark the correct person on the answer sheet.

61.   Who had visited USA and Germany?

62.   Who had visited USA and France?

63.   Who had visited Spain and Portugal?

64.   Who had visited France and Germany?

65.   Who had visited Spain and Germany?

In the following questions, there are two pairs of words. Only one of the five answers will go equally well with both pairs. Select the correct word and mark it on the answer sheet.

66.   (angry intersect)   (gruff meet)
       jam traverse cross annoyance tempered

67.   (trench hollow)   (abandon dump)
       moat discard excavation ditch pit

68.   (container chest)   (hit slap)
       accommodation box carton blow smack

69.   (authority influence)   (force strength)
       pressure prestige power position skill

70.   (elegant stylish)   (sting painful)
       smooth fashionable neat smart sharp

In the following questions, complete the sentences in the most sensible way. The alphabet is provided to help you. Mark the correct letters on the answer sheet.

A B C D E F G H I J K L M N O P Q R S T U V W X Y Z

71.   AB is to EF as FG is to ⎯⎯⎯⎯⎯⎯

72.   BD is to DG as JF is to ⎯⎯⎯⎯⎯⎯

73.   MN is to KP as PQ is to ⎯⎯⎯⎯⎯⎯

74.   GH is to JF as RS is to ⎯⎯⎯⎯⎯⎯

75.   TU is to YQ as JK is to ⎯⎯⎯⎯⎯⎯

In the following questions, one of the words in each bracket is either almost the same or almost the opposite of the word outside the brackets. Mark the correct word on the answer sheet.

76.   REAL   (alive imagine actual impossible thing)

77.   EXTEND   (alter enlarge intend extract maintain)

78.   ANGER   (attack sorrow cruelty hatred wrath)

79.   HASTE   (agility rush enthusiasm willingness urge)

80.   NEAR   (inside here beyond further distant)

Anthem Test Papers
11+ and 12+ Verbal Reasoning Book 1
Answer Sheet 5

Please select your answers by filling in the correct boxes.

Name:

1
- S ☐
- W ☐
- E ☐
- A ☐
- T ☐

2
- F ☐
- R ☐
- I ☐
- E ☐
- D ☐

3
- F ☐
- R ☐
- S ☐
- T ☐
- Y ☐

4
- T ☐
- R ☐
- A ☐
- S ☐
- H ☐

5
- C ☐
- R ☐
- A ☐
- V ☐
- E ☐

6
- P ☐
- B ☐
- H ☐
- K ☐
- T ☐

7
- B ☐
- E ☐
- L ☐
- M ☐
- F ☐

8
- O ☐
- B ☐
- E ☐
- D ☐
- S ☐

9
- B ☐
- S ☐
- M ☐
- G ☐
- C ☐

10
- P ☐
- D ☐
- T ☐
- W ☐
- L ☐

11
- OR ☐
- QR ☐
- PR ☐
- PQ ☐
- PS ☐

12
- SS ☐
- US ☐
- TR ☐
- TT ☐
- TS ☐

13
- EW ☐
- DW ☐
- GW ☐
- DV ☐
- DX ☐

14
- VE ☐
- XE ☐
- WD ☐
- WE ☐
- WF ☐

15
- BD ☐
- ED ☐
- FD ☐
- EF ☐
- ES ☐

16
- neat ☐ | tumble ☐
- rough ☐ | diamond ☐
- humble ☐ | smooth ☐

17
- fake ☐ | expensive ☐
- sale ☐ | real ☐
- object ☐ | antique ☐

18
- relaxed ☐ | tense ☐
- soothing ☐ | awake ☐
- gentle ☐ | astute ☐

19
- come ☐ | steady ☐
- enter ☐ | go ☐
- ready ☐ | door ☐

20
- jittery ☐ | nervous ☐
- springy ☐ | jumpy ☐
- energetic ☐ | calm ☐

21
- The football ☐
- football team ☐
- team is ☐
- is now ☐
- playing well ☐

22
- Fire broke ☐
- broke out ☐
- out and ☐
- and panic ☐
- panic ensued ☐

23
- David threw ☐
- threw ink ☐
- ink cartridges ☐
- cartridges in ☐
- the bin ☐

24
- The naughty ☐
- naughty baby ☐
- baby threw ☐
- threw the ☐
- the bottle ☐

25
- The white ☐
- white markings ☐
- markings could ☐
- could easily ☐
- easily be ☐

26
- hard ☐ | time ☐
- different ☐ | late ☐
- easy ☐ | hurry ☐

27
- jump ☐ | shirt ☐
- hop ☐ | knot ☐
- finish ☐ | undo ☐

28
- failure ☐ | neat ☐
- examination ☐ | smooth ☐
- money ☐ | coarse ☐

29
- serious ☐ | swim ☐
- toys ☐ | sink ☐
- infant ☐ | water ☐

30
- leaves ☐ | narrow ☐
- autumn ☐ | crowded ☐
- tumble ☐ | fitness ☐

31
- RHNF ☐
- RHMF ☐
- RHMG ☐
- RGMF ☐
- RHMP ☐

32
- FOUR ☐
- FORT ☐
- FOND ☐
- FORK ☐
- FOUL ☐

33
- TDTY ☐
- TDXU ☐
- TDXT ☐
- TDTX ☐
- TDXS ☐

34
- SKIP ☐
- SKIM ☐
- SKIN ☐
- SKID ☐
- SHIN ☐

35
- HJQV ☐
- HJQX ☐
- HKQU ☐
- HJQU ☐
- HKQV ☐

36
- 15 ☐
- 22 ☐
- 30 ☐
- 23 ☐
- 11 ☐

37
- 3 ☐
- 12 ☐
- 30 ☐
- 45 ☐
- 60 ☐

38
- 13 ☐
- 18 ☐
- 26 ☐
- 36 ☐
- 72 ☐

39
- 12 ☐
- 14 ☐
- 23 ☐
- 26 ☐
- 32 ☐

40
- 12 ☐
- 14 ☐
- 16 ☐
- 32 ☐
- 36 ☐

Answer Sheet 5

Please select your answers by
filling in the correct boxes.

41
SING ☐
SANE ☐
SOLE ☐
SANG ☐
SIGN ☐

42
DOPE ☐
DOLL ☐
DOVE ☐
DOWN ☐
DULL ☐

43
LINE ☐
LIFE ☐
LIFT ☐
LINT ☐
LOFT ☐

44
TIDE ☐
TIER ☐
TILE ☐
TIDY ☐
TIME ☐

45
MIST ☐
MAST ☐
FAST ☐
FIST ☐
MUST ☐

46
MOON ☐ PARK ☐
SPACE ☐ LIGHT ☐
DARK ☐ LEFT ☐

47
YELLOW ☐ PAINT ☐
BLACK ☐ SKY ☐
RED ☐ BERRY ☐

48
THUNDER ☐ LOCK ☐
RAIN ☐ BOLT ☐
STORM ☐ LEVER ☐

49
BEETLE ☐ KNEES ☐
ANT ☐ HIVE ☐
BEE ☐ ROOM ☐

50
PINK ☐ LIP ☐
ROSE ☐ STUD ☐
CORAL ☐ BUD ☐

51
finger ☐
ear ☐
rib ☐
thumb ☐
tooth ☐

52
flight ☐
fright ☐
scare ☐
swear ☐
stare ☐

53
collapse ☐
flow ☐
build ☐
fall ☐
water ☐

54
enemy ☐
neighbour ☐
competitor ☐
ally ☐
foe ☐

55
petty ☐
pretty ☐
attractive ☐
attentive ☐
perfect ☐

56
5035 ☐
0351 ☐
0503 ☐
2503 ☐
1052 ☐

57
5035 ☐
0351 ☐
0503 ☐
2503 ☐
1052 ☐

58
5035 ☐
0351 ☐
0503 ☐
2503 ☐
1052 ☐

59
5035 ☐
0351 ☐
0503 ☐
2503 ☐
1052 ☐

60
5 ☐
6 ☐
7 ☐
8 ☐
9 ☐

61
round ☐
world ☐
oval ☐
ball ☐
disco ☐

62
abandon ☐
renounce ☐
cancel ☐
surrender ☐
depart ☐

63
sketch ☐
undertaking ☐
operation ☐
effort ☐
act ☐

64
payment ☐
strike ☐
raid ☐
charge ☐
attack ☐

65
element ☐
part ☐
scrap ☐
share ☐
unit ☐

66
4 ☐
5 ☐
10 ☐
12 ☐
14 ☐

67
28 ☐
38 ☐
40 ☐
44 ☐
46 ☐

68
40 ☐
50 ☐
62 ☐
69 ☐
100 ☐

69
22 ☐
23 ☐
24 ☐
30 ☐
38 ☐

70
208 ☐
324 ☐
334 ☐
486 ☐
586 ☐

71
STOP ☐
WANT ☐
SWOT ☐
WASP ☐
PANT ☐

72
TRAP ☐
RAPT ☐
CARP ☐
CART ☐
ROTA ☐

73
RAIL ☐
FILM ☐
MAIN ☐
FOIL ☐
MAIL ☐

74
VEIL ☐
TILE ☐
VOTE ☐
WOVE ☐
HIVE ☐

75
ROOF ☐
FAME ☐
FORM ☐
FEAR ☐
FARE ☐

76
ship ☐
yacht ☐
pier ☐
harbour ☐
boat ☐

77
uncle ☐
sister ☐
father ☐
daughter ☐
niece ☐

78
lead ☐
follow ☐
pursue ☐
iron ☐
tail ☐

79
whirled ☐
world ☐
swirled ☐
twirled ☐
earth ☐

80
scales ☐
feathers ☐
bone ☐
fur ☐
blood ☐

Test Paper 5

In the following questions, one letter can be moved from the word on the left to the word on the right to form two new words. The letter may be removed from any position in the first word and placed in any position in the second word. No other letters may be rearranged. Mark the correct letter on the answer sheet.

1.   SWEAT   HEN

2.   FRIEND   FIST

3.   FROSTY   EARL

4.   TRASH   HEIR

5.   CRAVE   SPOT

In the questions below, the same letter must fit in both sets of brackets to complete the word in front of the brackets and begin the word after the brackets. Mark the correct letter on the answer sheet.

6.   SIC   ()   ICK   SIL   ()   ISS

7.   SEL   ()   ELT   TIF   ()   UME

8.   HER   ()   VEN   FIV   ()   XIT

9.   FAN   ()   OAT   GON   ()   ONE

10.   QUI   ()   RIP   FEL   ()   WIN

In the following questions, find the letters that will complete the sentence in the most sensible way. The alphabet is provided to help you. Mark the correct letters on the answer sheet.

A B C D E F G H I J K L M N O P Q R S T U V W X Y Z

11.   DF is to HJ as LN is to _____

12.   ZY is to XW as VU is to _____

13.   AZ is to BY as CX is to _____

14.   RS is to UV as TB is to _____

15.   NO is to QR as BA is to _____

In the following questions, find the two words, one from each set of brackets, that are the most opposite in meaning. Mark the correct words on the answer sheet.

16.   (neat rough humble)   (tumble diamond smooth)

17.   (fake sale object)   (expensive real antique)

18.   (relaxed soothing gentle)   (tense awake astute)

19.   (come enter ready)   (steady go door)

20.   (jittery springy energetic) (nervous jumpy calm)

In the following questions, a four-letter word can be formed from the letters at the end of one word and the beginning of the next, without changing the order of the letters. Find the pair of words and mark it on the answer sheet.

21.   The football team is now playing well.

22.   Fire broke out and panic ensued.

23.   David threw ink cartridges in the bin.

24.   The naughty baby threw the bottle.

25.   The white markings could easily be seen.

In the following questions, find the two words, one from each set of brackets, that will complete the sentence in the most sensible way. Mark the correct words on the answer sheet.

26.   Difficult is to (hard, different, easy) as early is to (time, late, hurry).

27.   Start is to (jump, hop, finish) as tie is to (shirt, knot, undo).

28.   Success is to (failure, examination, money) as rough is to (neat, smooth, coarse).

29.   Playful is to (serious, toys, infant) as float is to (swim, sink, water).

30.   Fall is to (leaves, autumn, tumble) as cramped is to (narrow, crowded, fitness).

In the following questions, a different code is used for each question. The first word has been worked out for you. Work out the second word, using the same code. The alphabet is provided to help you. Mark the correct word on the answer sheet.

A B C D E F G H I J K L M N O P Q R S T U V W X Y Z

31.   If PLAY is represented in code by OKZX what is SING in the same code?

32.   If GOAL is represented in code by IMCJ what does HMWJ represent?

33.   If ARENA is represented in code by XTDQX what is REAR in the same code?

34.   If GCLV represents FAIR in code what does TMLR represent?

35.   If MAGIC is represented in code by OYIGE what is FLOW in the same code?

In the following questions, the three numbers in each group are related in the same way. Find the number that completes the last group. Mark the correct number on the answer sheet.

36.   6 (12) 3   5 (25) 10   7 ( ) 8

37.   8 (15) 22   6 (15) 24   15 ( ) 45

38.   3 (27) 9   5 (35) 7   9 ( ) 4

39.   2 (7) 3   5 (14) 4   6 ( ) 20

40.   8 (20) 4   9 (24) 6   6 ( ) 2

In the following questions, the first word is changed into the last word by replacing one letter at a time with a different letter, in a total of three replacement steps. Two new words are formed in the intermediate steps. Mark the two new words on the answer sheet.

41.   SALE   42.   DOLE   43.   LONE   44.   TAME   45.   FISH

        - - - -   - - - -   - - - -   - - - -   - - - -

        - - - -   - - - -   - - - -   - - - -   - - - -

        SONG   DUEL   LILT   TIDY   MINT

In the following questions, one of the words from the bracket on the left can be joined to a word from the bracket on the right to form a completely new and proper word. Mark the two correct words on the answer sheet.

46.   (MOON SPACE DARK)   (PARK LIGHT LEFT)

47.   (YELLOW BLACK RED)   (PAINT SKY BERRY)

48.   (THUNDER RAIN STORM)   (LOCK BOLT LEVER)

49.   (BEETLE ANT BEE)   (KNEES HIVE ROOM)

50.   (PINK ROSE CORAL)   (LIP STUD BUD)

In the following questions, find the two words from each set of words that are the most similar in meaning. Mark the correct words on the answer sheet.

51.   finger ear rib thumb tooth

52.   flight fright scare swear stare

53.   collapse flow build fall water

54.   enemy neighbour competitor ally foe

55.   petty pretty attractive attentive perfect

In the following questions, the words PRAM, MARE, REAP, AREA and RARE are represented by the codes 5035, 0351, 0503, 2503 and 1052 (in no particular order). Work out the code for each word and mark it on the answer sheet.

56.   PRAM

57.   MARE

58.   REAP

59.   RARE

60.   Lily is twice as old as Alice and seven years older than Ted. Last year Ted was four years old. How old will Alice be next year?

In the following questions, there are two pairs of words in brackets. Only one of the five answers will go equally well with both pairs. Select the correct word and mark it on the answer sheet.

61.   (globe party)   (sphere dance)
       round world oval ball disco

62.   (forgo evacuate)   (drop leave)
       abandon renounce cancel surrender depart

63.   (behave performance)   (conduct impersonate)
       sketch undertaking operation effort act

64.   (cost price)   (assault rush)
       payment strike raid charge attack

65.   (bit fraction)   (split leave)
       element part scrap share unit

In each of the following questions, find the number that continues the series in the most sensible way. Mark the correct number on the answer sheet.

66.   480   240   80   20   _____

67.   38   38   36   40   34   42   32   _____

68.   5   7   12   19   31   _____

69.   9   9   10   12   15   19   _____

70.   2   6   18   54   162   _____

In the following questions, there are two sets of words. The word in the brackets on the left hand side has been formed using some of the letters from the words on either side of the brackets. Form the missing word in the brackets on the right hand side from its pair of words, in the same way. Mark the newly formed word on the answer sheet.

71.   CHIP   (ARCH)   WARD   :   SPOT   (   )   SWAN

72.   KILN   (MILK)   MOAT   :   PART   (   )   COAX

73.   RAFT   (DARK)   DUSK   :   LION   (   )   FARM

74.   PILL   (LIFT)   FEET   :   WITH   (   )   LOVE

75.   TAKE   (KILT)   TAIL   :   SAFE   (   )   MOOR

In the following questions, three of the five words are related in some way. Which two words do not belong with the three related words? Mark the correct words on the answer sheet.

76.   ship yacht pier harbour boat

77.   uncle sister father daughter niece

78.   lead follow pursue iron tail

79.   whirled world swirled twirled earth

80.   scales feathers bones fur blood

Anthem Test Papers
11+ and 12+ Verbal Reasoning Book 1
Answer Sheet 6

Please select your answers by filling in the correct boxes.

Name:

1 C ☐ O ☐ M ☐ E ☐ T ☐

2 S ☐ T ☐ I ☐ N ☐ K ☐

3 E ☐ V ☐ E ☐ R ☐ Y ☐

4 M ☐ E ☐ N ☐ T ☐ L ☐

5 R ☐ O ☐ U ☐ T ☐ S ☐

6 century ☐ date ☐ day ☐ decade ☐ millennium ☐

7 triangle ☐ circle ☐ rectangle ☐ square ☐ perimeter ☐

8 thick ☐ stout ☐ slender ☐ minute ☐ chunky ☐

9 hunt ☐ hide ☐ capture ☐ chase ☐ pursue ☐

10 adventure ☐ hazard ☐ accident ☐ danger ☐ risk ☐

11 NH ☐ NF ☐ NG ☐ MG ☐ OG ☐

12 N ☐ O ☐ Q ☐ P ☐ R ☐

13 PKO ☐ PKN ☐ PKM ☐ PLN ☐ OKN ☐

14 KH ☐ KF ☐ KG ☐ LG ☐ MG ☐

15 WX ☐ ZX ☐ YW ☐ YX ☐ YY ☐

16 Tom found ☐ found a ☐ a crab ☐ crab and ☐ jelly fish ☐

17 Pupils often ☐ often write ☐ write wrong ☐ wrong answers ☐ answers at ☐

18 Apples and ☐ and pears ☐ pears are ☐ are good ☐ for you ☐

19 The room ☐ room was ☐ was full ☐ of noisy ☐ noisy people ☐

20 The candles ☐ candles shone ☐ shone brightly ☐ brightly in ☐ the dark ☐

21 danger ☐ sadness ☐ fear ☐ feeling ☐ trouble ☐ emotion ☐

22 four ☐ twelve ☐ eight ☐ fifteen ☐ sixteen ☐ twenty-eight ☐

23 accident ☐ clown ☐ theatre ☐ funny ☐ sad ☐ joke ☐

24 trick ☐ article ☐ caught ☐ bought ☐ trap ☐ shop ☐

25 window ☐ door ☐ beaker ☐ solid ☐ break ☐ forest ☐

26 DEAR ☐ REAL ☐ READ ☐ DALE ☐ DEAL ☐

27 ROAD ☐ BARD ☐ DRAB ☐ DARE ☐ ARAB ☐

28 STAR ☐ STIR ☐ ARTS ☐ RATS ☐ SITS ☐

29 ROD ☐ RED ☐ ONE ☐ DOE ☐ DEN ☐

30 LIT ☐ LOT ☐ POT ☐ PET ☐ PIT ☐

31 45 ☐ 46 ☐ 47 ☐ 48 ☐ 49 ☐

32 82 ☐ 84 ☐ 66 ☐ 64 ☐ 62 ☐

33 74 ☐ 75 ☐ 76 ☐ 77 ☐ 78 ☐

34 76 ☐ 82 ☐ 102 ☐ 104 ☐ 106 ☐

35 96 ☐ 107 ☐ 89 ☐ 82 ☐ 90 ☐

36 VY ☐ WY ☐ ZX ☐ ZA ☐ ZY ☐

37 JX ☐ HX ☐ IY ☐ IW ☐ IX ☐

38 WG ☐ XF ☐ WF ☐ WG ☐ WF ☐

39 NP ☐ NM ☐ OL ☐ NL ☐ ML ☐

40 NX ☐ LY ☐ MX ☐ MY ☐ OY ☐

Answer Sheet 6

Please select your answers by
filling in the correct boxes.

41
- RTKOH ☐
- RTKOF ☐
- RTKNG ☐
- RTKOM ☐
- RTKOG ☐

42
- SCALE ☐
- SCARE ☐
- SCRAP ☐
- SCRUB ☐
- SCORE ☐

43
- MAKE ☐
- MAIL ☐
- MAID ☐
- MASK ☐
- MACE ☐

44
- MAIN ☐
- MALE ☐
- MADE ☐
- MARK ☐
- MAST ☐

45
- SHIN ☐
- SHOT ☐
- SHOW ☐
- SHAM ☐
- SHOP ☐

46
- P ☐
- R ☐
- H ☐
- W ☐
- S ☐

47
- E ☐
- T ☐
- D ☐
- P ☐
- W ☐

48
- D ☐
- K ☐
- B ☐
- L ☐
- T ☐

49
- N ☐
- B ☐
- T ☐
- L ☐
- M ☐

50
- N ☐
- R ☐
- D ☐
- M ☐
- L ☐

51
- SPEAR ☐
- PEARS ☐
- SPARE ☐
- REAPS ☐
- PEERS ☐

52
- SPEAR ☐
- PEARS ☐
- SPARE ☐
- REAPS ☐
- PEERS ☐

53
- SPEAR ☐
- PEARS ☐
- SPARE ☐
- REAPS ☐
- PEERS ☐

54
- SPEAR ☐
- PEARS ☐
- SPARE ☐
- REAPS ☐
- PEERS ☐

55
- 175 ☐
- 180 ☐
- 185 ☐
- 190 ☐
- 195 ☐

56
- 10 ☐
- 28 ☐
- 36 ☐
- 52 ☐
- 62 ☐

57
- 32 ☐
- 40 ☐
- 44 ☐
- 56 ☐
- 88 ☐

58
- 13 ☐
- 18 ☐
- 20 ☐
- 21 ☐
- 40 ☐

59
- 2 ☐
- 7 ☐
- 22 ☐
- 34 ☐
- 44 ☐

60
- 9 ☐
- 13 ☐
- 20 ☐
- 23 ☐
- 40 ☐

61
- A ☐
- B ☐
- C ☐
- D ☐
- F ☐

62
- A ☐
- B ☐
- C ☐
- D ☐
- F ☐

63
- A ☐
- B ☐
- C ☐
- D ☐
- F ☐

64
- A ☐
- B ☐
- C ☐
- D ☐
- F ☐

65
- A ☐
- B ☐
- C ☐
- D ☐
- F ☐

66
- frugal ☐
- waste ☐
- spend ☐
- extravagant ☐
- plentiful ☐
- palatial ☐

67
- courageous ☐
- timid ☐
- hero ☐
- fortitude ☐
- award ☐
- cowardly ☐

68
- cheer ☐
- applaud ☐
- mock ☐
- encourage ☐
- credit ☐
- award ☐

69
- possible ☐
- outcome ☐
- compatible ☐
- credible ☐
- result ☐
- improbable ☐

70
- mourn ☐
- sad ☐
- sorry ☐
- regret ☐
- sympathise ☐
- rejoice ☐

71
- delay ☐
- drought ☐
- belief ☐
- delude ☐
- deluge ☐
- postpone ☐

72
- disturbed ☐
- calm ☐
- fierce ☐
- mild ☐
- despise ☐
- haste ☐

73
- athletic ☐
- race ☐
- hastily ☐
- winner ☐
- speedily ☐
- victory ☐

74
- demolish ☐
- collapse ☐
- disaster ☐
- building ☐
- earthquake ☐
- destroy ☐

75
- evade ☐
- approach ☐
- proximity ☐
- direction ☐
- distance ☐
- avoid ☐

76
- beach ☐
- exceptionally ☐
- with ☐
- crowded ☐
- holidaymakers ☐

77
- The ☐
- pupils ☐
- enjoyed ☐
- all ☐
- lesson ☐

78
- The ☐
- coach ☐
- travelled ☐
- group ☐
- rail ☐

79
- days ☐
- had ☐
- not ☐
- been ☐
- sun ☐

80
- waves ☐
- sailed ☐
- across ☐
- choppy ☐
- yacht ☐

Test Paper 6

In the following questions, one letter can be moved from the word on the left to the word on the right to form two new words. The letter may be removed from any position in the first word and placed in any position in the second word. No other letters may be rearranged. Mark the correct letter on the answer sheet.

1. COMET   SING

2. STINK   MEAL

3. EVERY   CRATE

4. MENTAL   SAIL

5. ROUT   SIT

In the following questions, three of the five words are related in some way. Which two words do not belong with the three related words? Mark the correct words on the answer sheet.

6. century date day decade millennium

7. triangle circle rectangle square perimeter

8. thick stout slender minute chunky

9. hunt hide capture chase pursue

10. adventure hazard accident danger risk

In the following questions, find the letter or letters that continue(s) the series in the most sensible way. The alphabet is provided to help you. Mark the correct letter(s) on the answer sheet.

A B C D E F G H I J K L M N O P Q R S T U V W X Y Z

11. BC   ED   HE   KF   _____

12. A   B   D   G   K   _____

13. DCR   GEQ   JGP   MIO   _____

14. CO   EM   GK   II   _____

15. HI   ML   NO   SR   TU   _____

In the following questions, a four-letter word can be formed from the letters at the end of one word and the beginning of the next, without changing the order of the letters. Find the pair of words and mark it on the answer sheet.

16.   Tom found a crab and a jelly fish.

17.   Pupils often write wrong answers at first.

18.   Apples and pears are good for you.

19.   The room was full of noisy people.

20.   The candles shone brightly in the dark.

In the following questions, find the two words, one from each set of brackets, that will complete the sentence in the most sensible way. Mark the correct words on the answer sheet.

21.   Terror is to (danger, fear, trouble) as sorrow is to (sadness, feeling, emotion).

22.   Two is to (four, eight, sixteen) as three is to (twelve, fifteen, twenty-eight).

23.   Tragedy is to (accident, theatre, sad) as comedy is to (clown, funny, joke).

24.   Catch is to (trick, caught, trap) as buy is to (article, bought, shop).

25.   Glass is to (window, beaker, break) as wood is to (door, solid, forest).

In the following questions, there are three pairs of words. Find the word that completes the last pair of words in the same way as in the first two pairs. Mark the correct word on the answer sheet.

26.   RANDOM   MOAN : CARPET   TEAR   :   LADDER _____

27.   PEARL   REAL   : BEATS   TEAS   :   BOARD   _____

28.   TABLE   TALE   : HOUSE   HOSE :   STAIR   _____

29.   TRAIL   LIT   : BRAIN   NIB   :   DONER   _____

30.   CREATE   CAT   : FELINE   FIN   :   POLITE   _____

In the following questions, find the number that continues the series in the most sensible way. Mark the correct number on the answer sheet.

31.   93   84   75   66   57   _____

32.   20   22   26   34   50   _____

33.   98   95   91   88   84   81   _____

34.   80   82   88   76   96   70   _____

35.   7   9   16   25   41   66   _____

In the following questions, complete the sentences in the most sensible way. The alphabet is provided to help you. Mark the correct letters on the answer sheet.

A B C D E F G H I J K L M N O P Q R S T U V W X Y Z

36.   BG is to XJ as DV is to _____

37.   FR is to CV as LT is to _____

38.   LU is to OS as TH is to _____

39.   EN is to AP as RJ is to _____

40.   EH is to DK as NV is to _____

In the following questions, a different code is used for each question. The first word has been worked out for you. Work out the second word, using the same code. The alphabet is provided to help you. Mark the correct word on the answer sheet.

A B C D E F G H I J K L M N O P Q R S T U V W X Y Z

41.   If BADGE is represented by DCFIG what represents PRIME in the same code?

42.   If CALF is represented by ACJH what word is represented by QEPCN?

43.   If SCREAM is represented by TXYZQR what word is represented by RQXZ?

44.   If SIGN is represented by RGDJ what word is represented by LYAA?

45.   If PALM is represented by QZML what word is represented by TGPO?

In the questions below, the same letter must fit in both sets of brackets to complete the word in front of the brackets and begin the word after the brackets. Mark the correct letter on the answer sheet.

46.   LAUG ( )   AND   WIS   ( )   AT

47.   GNA   ( )   AGE   CLA   ( )   ARM

48.   FAS   ( )   UNE   POR   ( )   ENT

49.   GOW   ( )   EAR   MEA   ( )   OTE

50.   REBE   ( )   EVER   LEVE   ( )   OCK

In the following questions, the words SPEAR, PEARS, SPARE, REAPS and PEERS have been coded into symbols. Match each set of symbols with its corresponding word. Mark the correct word on the answer sheet.

51. - ÷ ! ? X

52. X ? ! - ÷

53. ? ÷ ! – X

54. X ? ÷ ! –

55. In an examination, Peter obtained 35 more marks than Tom, who in turn obtained twice as many as Harry. If Harry's mark was 30, what was the total number of marks obtained by the three boys? Mark the correct number on the answer sheet.

In the following questions, the three numbers in each group are related in the same way. Find the number that completes the last group. Mark the correct number on the answer sheet.

56. 21 (17) 6   44 (58) 24   14 ( ) 24

57. 18 (19) 5   14 (27) 17   8 ( ) 40

58. 5 (16) 6   7 (20) 6   8 ( ) 5

59. 18 (16) 4   20 (17) 6   12 ( ) 10

60. 5 (13) 2   3 (21) 6   4 ( ) 5

In the following questions, A = 10, B = 2, C = 3, D = 15, and F = 5. Work out the values of the following, giving your answer as a letter. Mark the correct letter on the answer sheet.

61. $\dfrac{A}{B}$

62. $\dfrac{F + A}{C}$

63. $\dfrac{D + F}{B}$

64. BF + F

65. BA – F

In the following questions, find the two words, one from each set of brackets, that are the most opposite in meaning. Mark the correct words on the answer sheet.

66.   (frugal waste spend)   (extravagant plentiful palatial)

67.   (courageous timid hero)   (fortitude award cowardly)

68.   (cheer applaud mock)   (encourage credit award)

69.   (possible outcome compatible)   (credible result improbable)

70.   (mourn sad sorry)   (regret sympathise rejoice)

In the following questions, find the two words, one from each set of brackets, that are the closest in meaning. Mark the correct words on the answer sheet.

71.   (delay drought belief)   (delude deluge postpone)

72.   (disturbed calm fierce)   (mild despise haste)

73.   (athletic race hastily)   (winner speedily victory)

74.   (demolish collapse disaster)   (building earthquake destroy)

75.   (evade approach proximity)   (direction distance avoid)

In each of the following sentences, two words must exchange places for the sentence to make sense. Mark the two correct words on the answer sheet.

76.   The beach was exceptionally holidaymakers with crowded.

77.   The pupils was enjoyed by all the lesson.

78.   The coach travelled by group and rail.

79.   The days had not been seen for sun.

80.   The waves sailed across the choppy yacht.

Anthem Test Papers
11+ and 12+ Verbal Reasoning Book 1
Answer Sheet 7

Please select your answers by filling in the correct boxes.

Name:

1
UP ☐	STEP ☐
STILL ☐	WOOD ☐
ROT ☐	TEN ☐

2
WARD ☐	AGE ☐
MAN ☐	FOR ☐
SO ☐	OF ☐

3
RAN ☐	MEANT ☐
STATE ☐	BED ☐
STAB ☐	SOME ☐

4
BODY ☐	THING ☐
ALL ☐	PERSON ☐
NO ☐	SOME ☐

5
SNOW ☐	EVEN ☐
JUST ☐	DESSERT ☐
CREAM ☐	ICE ☐

6
| FACE ☐ |
| FAIL ☐ |
| FAIR ☐ |
| FARE ☐ |
| FADE ☐ |

7
| SPOTS ☐ |
| SPOKE ☐ |
| SPILT ☐ |
| SPOUT ☐ |
| SPORT ☐ |

8
| SOLE ☐ |
| SOIL ☐ |
| SOAK ☐ |
| SOFT ☐ |
| TOLD ☐ |

9
| FOND ☐ |
| FOUR ☐ |
| FOUL ☐ |
| FORM ☐ |
| FORD ☐ |

10
| APPAL ☐ |
| APPLY ☐ |
| APPLE ☐ |
| APART ☐ |
| ARRAY ☐ |

11
| The car ☐ |
| car was ☐ |
| was a ☐ |
| a cheap ☐ |
| cheap bargain ☐ |

12
| The brightly ☐ |
| brightly coloured ☐ |
| coloured umbrellas ☐ |
| could easily ☐ |
| be seen ☐ |

13
| The hard ☐ |
| hard working ☐ |
| working rowers ☐ |
| rowers were ☐ |
| the victors ☐ |

14
| An apple ☐ |
| apple adds ☐ |
| adds vitamins ☐ |
| vitamins to ☐ |
| your diet ☐ |

15
| The fielder ☐ |
| fielder must ☐ |
| must continually ☐ |
| continually watch ☐ |
| watch attentively ☐ |

16
| PO ☐ |
| MO ☐ |
| NO ☐ |
| NP ☐ |
| NM ☐ |

17
| PJ ☐ |
| PL ☐ |
| OK ☐ |
| QK ☐ |
| PK ☐ |

18
| GI ☐ |
| HI ☐ |
| FI ☐ |
| GJ ☐ |
| GK ☐ |

19
| XF ☐ |
| VF ☐ |
| WE ☐ |
| WF ☐ |
| WG ☐ |

20
| HG ☐ |
| IG ☐ |
| GF ☐ |
| FF ☐ |
| HF ☐ |

21
| HIT ☐ |
| THE ☐ |
| FIT ☐ |
| FAT ☐ |
| HAT ☐ |

22
| REAR ☐ |
| HARE ☐ |
| HEAR ☐ |
| HEAD ☐ |
| DEAR ☐ |

23
| BULB ☐ |
| BELL ☐ |
| BALL ☐ |
| BILL ☐ |
| BULK ☐ |

24
| INN ☐ |
| GIN ☐ |
| RIG ☐ |
| RUG ☐ |
| MUG ☐ |

25
| DUSK ☐ |
| DUTY ☐ |
| DUMP ☐ |
| DUST ☐ |
| DUMB ☐ |

26
| N ☐ |
| M ☐ |
| P ☐ |
| Q ☐ |
| R ☐ |

27
| H ☐ |
| I ☐ |
| J ☐ |
| K ☐ |
| L ☐ |

28
| GE ☐ |
| HE ☐ |
| FE ☐ |
| FF ☐ |
| FG ☐ |

29
| LX ☐ |
| MX ☐ |
| KY ☐ |
| KW ☐ |
| KX ☐ |

30
| FE ☐ |
| CE ☐ |
| DF ☐ |
| DE ☐ |
| DG ☐ |

31
| 24 ☐ |
| 27 ☐ |
| 30 ☐ |
| 33 ☐ |
| 36 ☐ |

32
| 45 ☐ |
| 46 ☐ |
| 50 ☐ |
| 60 ☐ |
| 80 ☐ |

33
| 92 ☐ |
| 122 ☐ |
| 126 ☐ |
| 136 ☐ |
| 184 ☐ |

34
| 4•5 ☐ |
| 4•0 ☐ |
| 3 ☐ |
| 2•5 ☐ |
| 2 ☐ |

35
| 2 ☐ |
| 1•5 ☐ |
| 1 ☐ |
| 0•5 ☐ |
| 0 ☐ |

36
| 14 ☐ |
| 19 ☐ |
| 45 ☐ |
| 50 ☐ |
| 55 ☐ |

37
| 12 ☐ |
| 16 ☐ |
| 20 ☐ |
| 28 ☐ |
| 32 ☐ |

38
| 12 ☐ |
| 28 ☐ |
| 36 ☐ |
| 40 ☐ |
| 48 ☐ |

39
| 32 ☐ |
| 40 ☐ |
| 56 ☐ |
| 64 ☐ |
| 74 ☐ |

40
| 3 ☐ |
| 4 ☐ |
| 6 ☐ |
| 12 ☐ |
| 15 ☐ |

41
| A ☐ |
| B ☐ |
| C ☐ |
| D ☐ |
| E ☐ |

42
| A ☐ |
| B ☐ |
| C ☐ |
| D ☐ |
| E ☐ |

43
| A ☐ |
| B ☐ |
| C ☐ |
| D ☐ |
| E ☐ |

44
| A ☐ |
| B ☐ |
| C ☐ |
| D ☐ |
| E ☐ |

45
| A ☐ |
| B ☐ |
| C ☐ |
| D ☐ |
| E ☐ |

Answer Sheet 7

Please select your answers by filling in the correct boxes.

46

wet	☐	enough	☐
water	☐	food	☐
shortage	☐	scarce	☐

47

ill	☐	strength	☐
weakness	☐	strong	☐
healthy	☐	wealthy	☐

48

fruit	☐	fire	☐
round	☐	black	☐
tree	☐	fuel	☐

49

glove	☐	stop	☐
continue	☐	succeed	☐
cease	☐	start	☐

50

glove	☐	wood	☐
tree	☐	sock	☐
palm	☐	sole	☐

51

hard	☐	soft	☐
spike	☐	solid	☐
metal	☐	liquid	☐

52

fatigue	☐	weariness	☐
idleness	☐	exertion	☐
work	☐	rest	☐

53

humidity	☐	ice	☐
cold	☐	thaw	☐
melt	☐	snow	☐

54

outcome	☐	result	☐
game	☐	possible	☐
race	☐	win	☐

55

attack	☐	defend	☐
reprisal	☐	assault	☐
army	☐	retreat	☐

56

white	☐
dark	☐
pink	☐
bright	☐
red	☐

57

pond	☐
mountain	☐
mound	☐
hill	☐
lake	☐

58

two	☐
second	☐
third	☐
first	☐
four	☐

59

ice	☐
cold	☐
water	☐
steam	☐
warm	☐

60

modern	☐
today	☐
historic	☐
tomorrow	☐
pre-historic	☐

61

HIM	☐
BIT	☐
ARM	☐
CAN	☐
BAT	☐

62

SAT	☐
PIT	☐
HAT	☐
GET	☐
ARM	☐

63

EVE	☐
HAD	☐
PAN	☐
OUR	☐
ARE	☐

64

BAT	☐
SET	☐
NET	☐
SIP	☐
KIN	☐

65

SAP	☐
BIT	☐
ARE	☐
FAD	☐
BAT	☐

66

B	☐
A	☐
L	☐
D	☐

67

C	☐
A	☐
D	☐
G	☐
E	☐

68

T	☐
H	☐
R	☐
E	☐
A	☐

69

L	☐
E	☐
A	☐
D	☐

70

C	☐
A	☐
N	☐
O	☐
E	☐

71

L	☐
E	☐
M	☐
S	☐
D	☐

72

R	☐
P	☐
S	☐
T	☐
B	☐

73

T	☐
P	☐
B	☐
S	☐
W	☐

74

Y	☐
T	☐
E	☐
D	☐
A	☐

75

T	☐
C	☐
P	☐
M	☐
N	☐

76

miserly	☐	barter	☐
keep	☐	start	☐
prevent	☐	generous	☐

77

base	☐	building	☐
foundation	☐	attack	☐
surround	☐	summit	☐

78

display	☐	demonstration	☐
decline	☐	interior	☐
banner	☐	increase	☐

79

tangle	☐	harmony	☐
peace	☐	clarify	☐
confuse	☐	agreement	☐

80

care	☐	nuisance	☐
annoyance	☐	neglect	☐
noise	☐	forward	☐

Test Paper 7

In the following questions, one of the words from the bracket on the left can be joined to a word from the bracket on the right to form a completely new and proper word. Mark the two correct words on the answer sheet.

1. (UP STILL ROT) (STEP WOOD TEN)

2. (WARD MAN SO) (AGE FOR OF)

3. (RAN STATE STAB) (MEANT BED SOME)

4. (BODY ALL NO) (THING PERSON SOME)

5. (SNOW JUST CREAM) (EVEN DESSERT ICE)

In the following questions, a different code is used for each question. The first word has been worked out for you. Work out the second word, using the same code. The alphabet is provided to help you. Mark the correct word on the answer sheet.

A B C D E F G H I J K L M N O P Q R S T U V W X Y Z

6. If the code for ROSE is TQUG what does HCFG represent?

7. If the code for ROUND is SQXRI what does TRROJ represent?

8. If the code for THIN is VJKP what does VQNF represent?

9. If the code for RUIN is TSKL what does HMWP represent?

10. If the code for SHIRT is UFKPV was does CNRJG represent?

In the following sentences, a four-letter word can be formed from the letters at the end of one word and the beginning of the next, without changing the order of the letters. Find the hidden word and mark it on the answer sheet.

11. The car was a cheap bargain.

12. The brightly coloured umbrella could easily be seen.

13. The hard working rowers were the victors.

14. An apple adds vitamins to your diet.

15. The fielder must continually watch attentively.

In the following questions, find the letters that complete the sentences in the most sensible way. The alphabet is provided to help you. Mark the correct letters on the answer sheet.

A B C D E F G H I J K L M N O P Q R S T U V W X Y Z

16.   EN is to CL as PQ is to _____

17.   GK is to JH as MN is to _____

18.   TV is to UX as FG is to _____

19.   ST is to OX as AB is to _____

20.   MO is to NN as FG is to _____

In the following questions, there are three pairs of words. Find the word that completes the last pair of words in the same way as in the first two pairs. Mark the correct word on the answer sheet.

21.   PLANT   TAP   :   TEACH   HAT   :   THIEF   _____

22.   RATE   AT   :   ENAMEL   NAME   :   SHARED   _____

23.   PULL   PULP   :   TILL   TILT   :   BULL   _____

24.   GOOD   ODD   :   REAL   ALL   :   GRIN   _____

25.   SHOP   POSH   :   STOP   POST   :   STUD   _____

In the following questions, find the letter or letters that continue(s) the series in the most sensible way. The alphabet is provided to help you. Mark the correct letter(s) on the answer sheet.

A B C D E F G H I J K L M N O P Q R S T U V W X Y Z

26.   Z   V   S   Q   P   _____

27.   A   E   D   H   G   K   _____

28.   NM   QP   TS   WV   ZY   CB   _____

29.   AN   CP   ER   GT   IV   _____

30.   ST   PQ   MN   JK   GH   _____

In the following questions, find the number that continues the series in the most sensible way. Mark the correct number on the answer sheet.

31.   2   5   9   14   20   —————

32.   5   10   20   35   55   —————

33.   2   6   14   30   62   —————

34.   15·5   13   10·5   8   5·5   —————

35.   243   81   27   9   3   —————

In the following questions, the three numbers in each group are related in the same way. Find the number that completes the last group. Mark the correct number on the answer sheet.

36.   5 (24) 4   6 (21) 3   9 ( ) 5

37.   7 (67) 20   4 (49) 15   4 ( ) 8

38.   10 (20) 8   16 (16) 4   8 ( ) 20

39.   20 (35) 5   15 (27) 3   24 ( ) 8

40.   18 (3) 2   36 (2) 6   60 ( ) 5

In the following questions, A = 8, B = 7, C = 4, D = 3, and E = 12. Work out the values of the following, giving your answer as a letter. Mark the correct letter on the answer sheet.

41.   C + D

42.   (B – D) × D

43. $\dfrac{E}{C}$

44.   (C × D) – C

45.   CD – A

In the following questions, find the two words, one from each set of brackets, that will complete the sentence in the most sensible way. Mark the correct words on the answer sheet.

46.   Drought is to (wet, water, shortage) as famine is to (enough, food, scarce).

47.   Sickly is to (ill, weakness, healthy) as weak is to (strength, strong, wealthy).

48. Orange is to (fruit, round, tree) as coal is to (fire, black, fuel).

49. Commence is to (glove, continue, cease) as begin is to (stop, succeed, start).

50. Hand is to (glove, tree, palm) as foot is to (wood, sock, sole).

In the following questions, find the two words, one from each set of brackets, that are the closest in meaning. Mark the correct words on the answer sheet.

51. (hard spike metal) (soft solid liquid)

52. (fatigue idleness work) (weariness exertion rest)

53. (humidity cold melt) (ice thaw snow)

54. (outcome game race) (result possible win)

55. (attack reprisal army) (defend assault retreat)

In the following questions, three of the five words are related in some way. Which two words do not belong with the three related words? Mark the correct words on the answer sheet.

56. white dark pink bright red

57. pond mountain mound hill lake

58. two second third first four

59. ice cold water steam warm

60. modern today historic tomorrow pre-historic

In each of the following questions, the letters in capitals are missing three consecutive letters that can be inserted into the capital letters to form a word that completes the sentence. The three consecutive letters themselves form a sensible word. Mark the missing three-letter word on the answer sheet.

61. Although he slipped on the ice he was UNHED.

62. The restless pupil FIDED throughout the lesson.

63. He was advised NR to be late for work.

64. The TLES gave the young girl nasty stings.

65. There was a long DEE in Parliament.

In the following questions, one letter can be moved from the word on the left to the word on the right to form two new words. The letter may be removed from any position in the first word and placed in any position in the second word. No other letters may be rearranged. Mark the correct letter on the answer sheet.

66. BALD   DARING

67. CADGE   LAY

68. THREAT   SOW

69. LEAD   SIZE

70. CANOE   SHUT

In the questions below, the same letter must fit in both sets of brackets to complete the word in front of the brackets and begin the word after the brackets. Mark the correct letter on the answer sheet.

71. FIL () END   CAL () UCH

72. HEA () OLD   ME   () ALL

73. KER () AND   STA () OTH

74. NOS () ACH   FIN () ND

75. CLA () EAR   TRI () ART

In the following questions, find the two words, one from each set of brackets, that are the most opposite in meaning. Mark the correct words on the answer sheet.

76. (miserly keep prevent)   (barter start generous)

77. (base foundation surround)   (building attack summit)

78. (display decline banner)   (demonstration interior increase)

79. (tangle peace confuse)   (harmony clarify agreement)

80. (care annoyance noise)   (nuisance neglect forward)

Anthem Test Papers
11+ and 12+ Verbal Reasoning Book 1
Answer Sheet 8

Please select your answers by filling in the correct boxes.

Name:

1

OVER ☐	CAR ☐
OUT ☐	TERN ☐
PAT ☐	CAKE ☐

2

SO ☐	SLOW ☐
THIN ☐	ON ☐
FALL ☐	LANE ☐

3

SLOW ☐	HER ☐
FEAT ☐	HIGH ☐
BIG ☐	FIST ☐

4

MY ☐	HAT ☐
TALL ☐	NOR ☐
DO ☐	NOT ☐

5

HARD ☐	TEST ☐
FIT ☐	LAW ☐
INTELLIGENCE ☐	DONE ☐

6

| 60 ☐ |
| 72 ☐ |
| 84 ☐ |
| 96 ☐ |
| 110 ☐ |

7

| 46 ☐ |
| 47 ☐ |
| 48 ☐ |
| 49 ☐ |
| 50 ☐ |

8

| 14 ☐ |
| 15 ☐ |
| 16 ☐ |
| 17 ☐ |
| 22 ☐ |

9

| 15 ☐ |
| 16 ☐ |
| 17 ☐ |
| 18 ☐ |
| 22 ☐ |

10

| 10 ☐ |
| 13 ☐ |
| 14 ☐ |
| 24 ☐ |
| 27 ☐ |

11

| SIT ☐ |
| LIT ☐ |
| LOT ☐ |
| OIL ☐ |
| TOO ☐ |

12

| HER ☐ |
| ARE ☐ |
| BEE ☐ |
| ARC ☐ |
| FAR ☐ |

13

| ROBE ☐ |
| BORE ☐ |
| BOAT ☐ |
| BEAR ☐ |
| BARE ☐ |

14

| FINE ☐ |
| FAST ☐ |
| FIST ☐ |
| FIRE ☐ |
| FIRM ☐ |

15

| WING ☐ |
| WINS ☐ |
| WINE ☐ |
| SING ☐ |
| WIND ☐ |

16

| P ☐ |
| A ☐ |
| I ☐ |
| N ☐ |
| E ☐ |

17

| P ☐ |
| R ☐ |
| E ☐ |
| Y ☐ |

18

| B ☐ |
| E ☐ |
| A ☐ |
| R ☐ |

19

| B ☐ |
| R ☐ |
| O ☐ |
| W ☐ |

20

| T ☐ |
| H ☐ |
| E ☐ |
| R ☐ |
| E ☐ |

21

niece ☐	cousin ☐
mother ☐	relative ☐
woman ☐	man ☐

22

captain ☐	choir ☐
sport ☐	orchestra ☐
team ☐	tune ☐

23

stem ☐	wood ☐
seed ☐	trunk ☐
root ☐	leaf ☐

24

decade ☐	score ☐
tenth ☐	twentieth ☐
decimal ☐	percentage ☐

25

metric ☐	square ☐
cubic ☐	kilometre ☐
liquid ☐	length ☐

26

| FILL ☐ |
| FOIL ☐ |
| FIND ☐ |
| FOLD ☐ |
| SOLD ☐ |

27

| RULE ☐ |
| MULE ☐ |
| LUTE ☐ |
| LATE ☐ |
| LIMB ☐ |

28

| PAIL ☐ |
| MAIL ☐ |
| RAIL ☐ |
| SAIL ☐ |
| RIPS ☐ |

29

| ROLE ☐ |
| WORE ☐ |
| SOLE ☐ |
| SLOW ☐ |
| LOOK ☐ |

30

| SAND ☐ |
| LAND ☐ |
| SORE ☐ |
| WAND ☐ |
| SOLE ☐ |

31

| Examinations are ☐ |
| are not ☐ |
| not every ☐ |
| every pupils' ☐ |
| pupils' favourite ☐ |

32

| The athlete ☐ |
| athlete met ☐ |
| met the ☐ |
| the challenge ☐ |
| challenge successfully ☐ |

33

| What does ☐ |
| does she ☐ |
| she do ☐ |
| to annoy ☐ |
| annoy everybody ☐ |

34

| The inventor ☐ |
| inventor had ☐ |
| a good ☐ |
| good idea ☐ |
| idea rejected ☐ |

35

| The head ☐ |
| head said ☐ |
| said come ☐ |
| come at ☐ |
| my office ☐ |

36

| N ☐ |
| O ☐ |
| P ☐ |
| Q ☐ |
| R ☐ |

37

| I ☐ |
| J ☐ |
| K ☐ |
| L ☐ |
| M ☐ |

38

| Z ☐ |
| Y ☐ |
| W ☐ |
| X ☐ |
| V ☐ |

39

| NP ☐ |
| MO ☐ |
| NO ☐ |
| PO ☐ |
| NQ ☐ |

40

| UQ ☐ |
| SQ ☐ |
| TQ ☐ |
| TR ☐ |
| TP ☐ |

Answer Sheet 8

Please select your answers by filling in the correct boxes.

41 HMBS ☐ / HNBS ☐ / HNCS ☐ / HNBT ☐ / HMBT ☐

42 NAPE ☐ / NAME ☐ / NAGS ☐ / NOTE ☐ / NOSE ☐

43 OKQG ☐ / OKOG ☐ / OKPG ☐ / OKPH ☐ / OKPJ ☐

44 FOOL ☐ / FOOT ☐ / FOOD ☐ / FOND ☐ / FOLD ☐

45 FALL ☐ / FOAL ☐ / FOOD ☐ / FORD ☐ / FORM ☐

46 above ☐ high ☐ / under ☐ beneath ☐ / lie ☐ low ☐

47 act ☐ actual ☐ / real ☐ turn ☐ / dream ☐ imaginary ☐

48 journey ☐ by ☐ / home ☐ distant ☐ / near ☐ close ☐

49 lonely ☐ vacant ☐ / quiet ☐ solitary ☐ / peculiar ☐ noisy ☐

50 cruelty ☐ war ☐ / wealth ☐ kindness ☐ / hard ☐ manners ☐

51 P ☐ / K ☐ / N ☐ / T ☐ / D ☐

52 E ☐ / C ☐ / T ☐ / W ☐ / P ☐

53 E ☐ / B ☐ / T ☐ / M ☐ / Y ☐

54 D ☐ / F ☐ / T ☐ / W ☐ / M ☐

55 E ☐ / L ☐ / D ☐ / C ☐ / R ☐

56 hat ☐ / cap ☐ / beret ☐ / scarf ☐ / bonnet ☐

57 decide ☐ / search ☐ / investigate ☐ / examine ☐ / seek ☐

58 tree ☐ / bush ☐ / earth ☐ / grass ☐ / vegetable ☐

59 motorway ☐ / road ☐ / avenue ☐ / street ☐ / villa ☐

60 likelihood ☐ / certainty ☐ / chance ☐ / probability ☐ / opportunity ☐

61 1 ☐ / 15 ☐ / 22 ☐ / 23 ☐ / 56 ☐

62 15 ☐ / 20 ☐ / 25 ☐ / 30 ☐ / 60 ☐

63 13 ☐ / 17 ☐ / 22 ☐ / 36 ☐ / 40 ☐

64 14 ☐ / 16 ☐ / 26 ☐ / 32 ☐ / 46 ☐

65 22 ☐ / 30 ☐ / 44 ☐ / 56 ☐ / 66 ☐

66 QS ☐ / QQ ☐ / QR ☐ / PR ☐ / RR ☐

67 IM ☐ / IO ☐ / IN ☐ / HN ☐ / JN ☐

68 IW ☐ / GW ☐ / HV ☐ / HW ☐ / HX ☐

69 NV ☐ / OV ☐ / PV ☐ / PU ☐ / PT ☐

70 HF ☐ / HH ☐ / HG ☐ / GG ☐ / IG ☐

71 roar ☐ / thunder ☐ / clap ☐ / appreciation ☐ / ring ☐

72 mood ☐ / humour ☐ / cross ☐ / junction ☐ / crossroads ☐

73 perpendicular ☐ / design ☐ / erect ☐ / assemble ☐ / raise ☐

74 hobby ☐ / pleasure ☐ / game ☐ / challenge ☐ / tournament ☐

75 scrape ☐ / scrap ☐ / accurate ☐ / alter ☐ / mark ☐

76 entertain ☐ displease ☐ / happiness ☐ clown ☐ / delight ☐ amuse ☐

77 conflict ☐ courageous ☐ / hunted ☐ daunted ☐ / fearless ☐ afraid ☐

78 halt ☐ proceed ☐ / group ☐ collection ☐ / hobby ☐ individual ☐

79 promise ☐ indifferent ☐ / jealous ☐ trusting ☐ / secret ☐ envious ☐

80 warfare ☐ expose ☐ / protect ☐ assault ☐ / cover ☐ safeguard ☐

Test Paper 8

In the following questions, one of the words from the bracket on the left can be joined to a word from the bracket on the right to form a completely new and proper word. Mark the two correct words on the answer sheet.

1.   (OVER   OUT   PAT)   (CAR   TERN   CAKE)

2.   (SO   THIN   FALL)   (LOW   ON   LANE)

3.   (SLOW   FEAT   BIG)   (HER   HIGH   FIST)

4.   (MY   TALL   DO)   (HAT   NOR   NOT)

5.   (HARD   FIT   INTELLIGENCE)   (TEST   LAW   DONE)

In the following questions, find the number that continues the series in the most sensible way. Mark the correct number on the answer sheet.

6.   3   6   12   24   48   _____

7.   33   35   39   41   45   _____

8.   4   2   8   6   12   10   _____

9.   3   4   6   9   13   _____

10.   19   21   18   22   16   24   15   25   _____

In the following questions, there are three pairs of words. Find the word that completes the last pair of words in the same way as in the first two pairs. Mark the correct word on the answer sheet.

11.   TALES   ALE   :   TEARS   EAR   :   TOILS   _____

12.   WITH   WIT   :   SHAME   SAME   :   HARE   _____

13.   CARE   COAT   :   FLARE   FLOAT   :   BARE   _____

14.   FILE   LIFE   :   CARE   RACE   :   SIFT   _____

15.   YACHT   ACHE   :   SWORD   WORE   :   SWING   _____

In the following questions, one letter can be moved from the word on the left to the word on the right to form two new words. The letter may be removed from any position in the first word and placed in any position in the second word. No other letters may be rearranged. Mark the correct letter on the answer sheet.

16. PAINTED   BAT

17. PREY   CLAN

18. BEAR   LOW

19. BROW   TEAT

20. THERE   RUST

In the following questions, find the two words, one from each set of brackets, that will complete the sentence in the most sensible way. Mark the correct words on the answer sheet.

21. Aunt is to (niece mother woman) as uncle is to (cousin relative man).

22. Player is to (captain sport team) as singer is to (choir orchestra tune).

23. Plant is to (stem seed root) as tree is to (wood trunk leaf).

24. Ten is to (decade tenth decimal) as twenty is to (score twentieth percentage).

25. Litre is to (metric cubic liquid) as metre is to (square kilometre length).

In the following questions, there are two sets of words. The word in the brackets on the left hand side has been formed using some of the letters from the words on either side of the brackets. Form the missing word in the brackets on the right hand side from its pair of words, in the same way. Mark the newly formed word on the answer sheet.

26. DRUM   (DRAB)   ABLE   :   FOND   (   )   ILLS

27. SHUT   (HURT)   PART   :   BLUR   (   )   MITE

28. FAST   (SAIL)   BLIP   :   MART   (   )   SLIP

29. POST   (SPAN)   NAME   :   LOSE   (   )   WORK

30. BRAG   (RAIN)   SINK   :   CLAW   (   )   ENDS

In the following questions, a four-letter word can be formed from the letters at the end of one word and the beginning of the next, without changing the order of the letters. Find the pair of words and mark it on the answer sheet.

31.   Examinations are not every pupils' favourite.

32.   The athlete met the challenge successfully.

33.   What does she do to annoy everybody?

34.   The inventor had a good idea rejected.

35.   The head said, "Come at once to my office."

In the following questions, find the letter or letters that continue(s) the series in the most sensible way. The alphabet is provided to help you. Mark the correct letter(s) on the answer sheet.

A B C D E F G H I J K L M N O P Q R S T U V W X Y Z

36.   A   Y   C   W   F   T J   _____

37.   Z   A   W   D   T   G Q   _____

38.   Q   O   L   H   C   _____

39.   BC   EF   HI   KL   _____

40.   DA   HE   LI   PM   _____

In the following questions, a different code is used for each question. The first word has been worked out for you. Work out the second word, using the same code. The alphabet is provided to help you. Mark the correct word on the answer sheet.

A B C D E F G H I J K L M N O P Q R S T U V W X Y Z

41.   If PLUM is represented in code by QKVL what is GOAT in the same code?

42.   If HATE is represented in code by HBVH what does NBOH represent in the same code?

43.   If COAL is represented in code by EQCN what is MINE in the same code?

44.   If HAND is represented in code by GYKZ what word is represented by EMLP?

45.   If SORT is represented in code by UMTR what word is represented by HMQB?

In the following questions, find the two words, one from each set of brackets, that are the most opposite in meaning. Mark the correct words on the answer sheet.

46.   (above under lie)   (high beneath low)

47.   (act real dream)   (actual turn imaginary)

48.   (journey home near)   (by distant close)

49.   (lonely quiet peculiar)   (vacant solitary noisy)

50.   (cruelty wealth hard)   (war kindness manners)

In the following questions, the same letter must fit in both sets of brackets to complete the word in front of the brackets and begin the word after the brackets. Mark the correct letter on the answer sheet.

51.   SEE   () OOK   BI   () EST

52.   CAS   () AR   PAN   () RACK

53.   CUR   () OTH   CRA   () ATH

54.   CO   () IND   TO   () IPE

55.   FIL   () AMP   FOO   () EFT

In the following questions, one word out of the five does not belong with the others. Find the word and mark it on the answer sheet.

56.   hat cap beret scarf bonnet

57.   decide search investigate examine seek

58.   tree bush earth grass vegetable

59.   motorway road avenue street villa

60.   likelihood certainty chance probability opportunity

In the following questions, the three numbers in each group are related in the same way. Find the number that completes the last group. Mark the correct number on the answer sheet.

61.   6 (12) 3   5 (25) 10   7 ( ) 8

62.   8 (15) 22   6 (15) 24   15 ( ) 45

63.   3 (27) 9   5 (35) 7   9 ( ) 4

64.　2 (7) 3　　　5 (14) 4　　　6 ( ) 20

65.　8 (24) 6　　　11 (33) 6　　　14 ( ) 8

In the following questions, find the letters that complete the sentences in the most sensible way. The alphabet is provided to help you. Mark the correct letters on the answer sheet.

A B C D E F G H I J K L M N O P Q R S T U V W X Y Z

66.　DF is to FH as OP is to ——————

67.　TU is to RW as KL is to ——————

68.　WY is to TB as KT is to ——————

69.　TB is to RE as RS is to ——————

70.　ML is to IH as LK is to ——————

In the following questions, there are two pairs of words in brackets. Only one of the five answers will go equally well with both pairs. Select the correct word and mark it on the answer sheet.

71.　(applaud slap)　　　　　(bang peal)
　　roar thunder clap appreciation ring

72.　(traverse irritable)　　　(intersecting annoyed)
　　mood humour cross junction crossroads

73.　(vertical construct)　　　(upright build)
　　perpendicular design erect assemble raise

74.　(amusement competition)　(pastime contest)
　　hobby pleasure game challenge tournament

75.　(scratch correct)　　　　(stain grade)
　　scrape scrap accurate alter mark

In the following questions, find the two words, one from each set of brackets, that are the closest in meaning. Mark the correct words on the answer sheet.

76.　(entertain happiness delight)　(displease clown amuse)

77.　(conflict hunted fearless)　(courageous daunted afraid)

78.　(halt group hobby)　(proceed collection individual)

79.　(promise jealous secret)　(indifferent trusting envious)

80.　(warfare protect cover)　(expose assault safeguard)

Anthem Test Papers
11+ and 12+ Verbal Reasoning Book 1
Answer Sheet 9

Please select your answers by filling in the correct boxes.

Name:

1
DOOR ☐
REST ☐
RATE ☐
ROTE ☐
RODE ☐

2
TAKE ☐
TAPE ☐
TASK ☐
TEAK ☐
STAB ☐

3
TRAP ☐
RAPS ☐
TART ☐
SPAR ☐
PAST ☐

4
MATE ☐
MEAT ☐
MEAL ☐
MARE ☐
YEAR ☐

5
SORE ☐
SOAR ☐
STAR ☐
SAME ☐
SOME ☐

6
BID ☐
AND ☐
SAD ☐
PAD ☐
CAD ☐

7
SIN ☐
PEN ☐
PIN ☐
TEN ☐
TON ☐

8
TON ☐
AND ☐
LAP ☐
END ☐
CAN ☐

9
TIN ☐
ARE ☐
CAR ☐
TEN ☐
PUT ☐

10
HAS ☐
THE ☐
NOR ☐
HEN ☐
SIN ☐

11
E ☐
H ☐
S ☐
B ☐
F ☐

12
L ☐
Y ☐
T ☐
W ☐
F ☐

13
T ☐
E ☐
S ☐
K ☐
T ☐

14
P ☐
D ☐
R ☐
L ☐
S ☐

15
E ☐
B ☐
L ☐
H ☐
R ☐

16
B ☐
L ☐
E ☐
N ☐
D ☐

17
C ☐
R ☐
E ☐
A ☐
T ☐

18
B ☐
E ☐
G ☐
A ☐
N ☐

19
R ☐
O ☐
B ☐
E ☐

20
S ☐
O ☐
F ☐
T ☐
E ☐

21
The ship ☐
ship only ☐
only sells ☐
sells kippers ☐
kippers on ☐

22
took years ☐
years to ☐
to discover ☐
discover aids ☐
for handicapped ☐

23
The calm ☐
calm endless ☐
endless sea ☐
sea disappeared ☐
disappeared on ☐

24
The rule ☐
rule has ☐
has always ☐
post early ☐
early for ☐

25
The report ☐
report was ☐
was received ☐
received proudly ☐
proudly by ☐

26
crooked ☐ zigzag ☐
tower ☐ minute ☐
colossal ☐ gigantic ☐

27
police ☐ criminal ☐
threaten ☐ stop ☐
market ☐ protect ☐

28
hobby ☐ trifling ☐
trivial ☐ work ☐
distress ☐ comfort ☐

29
exit ☐ original ☐
creative ☐ arrival ☐
polite ☐ discourteous ☐

30
savage ☐ retreat ☐
recede ☐ deduct ☐
increase ☐ multiply ☐

31
collection ☐
flowers ☐
bunch ☐
stamps ☐
gathering ☐

32
diminish ☐
magnify ☐
shrink ☐
dwindle ☐
divide ☐

33
authorise ☐
persist ☐
freedom ☐
permit ☐
allow ☐

34
turbulent ☐
thunderous ☐
raging ☐
subdued ☐
silent ☐

35
demolish ☐
construct ☐
destroy ☐
erect ☐
build ☐

36
DQPVD ☐
DQOVD ☐
DQPVE ☐
DRPVD ☐
DRPVE ☐

37
GCPH ☐
GCPJ ☐
GCPI ☐
GDPI ☐
GDIP ☐

38
BRAT ☐
BEAT ☐
BRAG ☐
BRIM ☐
BARE ☐

39
SOLD ☐
SOLE ☐
SOIL ☐
SOLO ☐
SALE ☐

40
READ ☐
DEAR ☐
DEED ☐
REED ☐
REAR ☐

Answer Sheet 9

Please select your answers by
filling in the correct boxes.

41
MO ☐
PO ☐
NP ☐
NO ☐
NQ ☐

42
TZ ☐
UZ ☐
SZ ☐
UY ☐
UW ☐

43
MR ☐
MT ☐
KS ☐
MS ☐
LS ☐

44
OY ☐
OZ ☐
NZ ☐
MZ ☐
OA ☐

45
UV ☐
TV ☐
SW ☐
SV ☐
SU ☐

46
5 ☐
11 ☐
13 ☐
14 ☐
29 ☐

47
24 ☐
33 ☐
66 ☐
99 ☐
122 ☐

48
32 ☐
40 ☐
48 ☐
64 ☐
80 ☐

49
35 ☐
45 ☐
58 ☐
78 ☐
90 ☐

50
30 ☐
60 ☐
120 ☐
240 ☐
480 ☐

51
565 ☐
660 ☐
664 ☐
665 ☐
666 ☐

52
2 ☐
3 ☐
4 ☐
6 ☐
1 ☐

53
67 ☐
69 ☐
81 ☐
91 ☐
101 ☐

54
24 ☐
25 ☐
26 ☐
27 ☐
41 ☐

55
11 ☐
12 ☐
13 ☐
24 ☐
25 ☐

56
U ☐
V ☐
W ☐
X ☐
Y ☐

57
F ☐
G ☐
H ☐
I ☐
J ☐

58
F ☐
G ☐
H ☐
L ☐
M ☐

59
PJ ☐
MJ ☐
NL ☐
NJ ☐
NK ☐

60
Q ☐
R ☐
S ☐
T ☐
U ☐

61
BOOTS ☐
BOAST ☐
TOAST ☐
STABS ☐
BOATS ☐

62
BOOTS ☐
BOAST ☐
TOAST ☐
STABS ☐
BOATS ☐

63
BOOTS ☐
BOAST ☐
TOAST ☐
STABS ☐
BOATS ☐

64
BOOTS ☐
BOAST ☐
TOAST ☐
STABS ☐
BOATS ☐

65
18 ☐
20 ☐
22 ☐
32 ☐
42 ☐

66
CARPET ☐ STAIR ☐
HIDE ☐ FITTING ☐
HIGH ☐ WAY ☐

67
ENGINE ☐ POWER ☐
IN ☐ TEND ☐
PORT ☐ CAR ☐

68
CARE ☐ GIVE ☐
BE ☐ FULL ☐
FORE ☐ AN ☐

69
PLEA ☐ GUILTY ☐
CRIME ☐ SURE ☐
REST ☐ ASSURED ☐

70
CARD ☐ PACK ☐
WARD ☐ ACE ☐
STAR ☐ ROBE ☐

71
flavour ☐ colour ☐
type ☐ appearance ☐
dissimilar ☐ matching ☐

72
adaptable ☐ steel ☐
light ☐ harsh ☐
electricity ☐ stiff ☐

73
weather ☐ time ☐
traffic ☐ jam ☐
late ☐ prompt ☐

74
relaxed ☐ angry ☐
smooth ☐ mood ☐
behaviour ☐ tense ☐

75
generous ☐ gale ☐
wind ☐ punish ☐
kind ☐ strict ☐

76
dictate ☐
demand ☐
direct ☐
responsible ☐
military ☐

77
punishment ☐
reward ☐
fine ☐
imposition ☐
assessment ☐

78
achievement ☐
great ☐
brilliant ☐
diligent ☐
meritorious ☐

79
tolerant ☐
unbiased ☐
respectful ☐
disciplined ☐
just ☐

80
fraction ☐
incomplete ☐
part ☐
responsible ☐
capacity ☐

Test Paper 9

In the following questions, there are two sets of words. The word in the brackets on the left hand side has been formed using some of the letters from the words on either side of the brackets. Form the missing word in the brackets on the right hand side from its pair of words, in the same way. Mark the newly formed word on the answer sheet.

1. LOOK (WALK) WANT : SOOT ( ) READ

2. PALM (LAMP) MAPS : PATS ( ) BAKE

3. BOOK (BOLD) LOUD : PART ( ) SPAT

4. STAMP (PART) ROAM : REALM ( ) TRAY

5. CAME (MICE) TIME : MOST ( ) HARE

In the following questions, the letters in capitals are missing three consecutive letters that can be inserted into the capital letters to form a word that completes the sentence. The three consecutive letters themselves form a sensible word. Mark the missing three-letter word on the answer sheet.

6. In the P.E. lesson all the pupils completed a HSTAND.

7. The judge gave the prisoner a long SENCE.

8. The plane DESCED smoothly on to the runway.

9. Netball matches are OF cancelled because of rain.

10. To avoid the traffic jam the driver took ANOR route.

In the following questions, the same letter must fit in both sets of brackets to complete the word in front of the brackets and begin the word after the brackets. Mark the correct letter on the answer sheet.

11. COM ( ) AKE : SCRU ( ) ILL

12. BEL ( ) RAP : TIL ( ) EAR

13. STAC ( ) NOW : MAS ( ) NIT

14. SOU ( ) AMP : LAPE ( ) AIR

15. CAS ( ) AND : PUS ( ) ARE

In the following questions, one letter can be moved from the word on the left to the word on the right to form two new words. The letter may be removed from any position in the first word and placed in any position in the second word. No other letters may be rearranged. Mark the correct letter on the answer sheet.

16. BLEND   PACE

17. CREATE   PLAN

18. BEGAN   ROW

19. ROBE   CAN

20. SOFTEN   DOE

In the following questions, a four-letter word can be formed from the letters at the end of one word and the beginning of the next, without changing the order of the letters. Find the hidden word and mark it on the answer sheet.

21. The ship only sells kippers on Friday.

22. It took years to discover aids for handicapped citizens.

23. The calm endless sea disappeared on the horizon.

24. The rule has always been post early for Christmas.

25. The report was received proudly by the pupil.

In the following questions, find the two words, one from each set of brackets, that are the most opposite in meaning. Mark the correct words on the answer sheet.

26. (crooked   tower   colossal)   (zigzag   minute   gigantic)

27. (police   threaten   market)   (criminal   stop   protect)

28. (hobby   trivial   distress)   (trifling   work   comfort)

29. (exit   creative   polite)   (original   arrival   discourteous)

30. (savage   recede   increase)   (retreat   deduct   multiply)

In the following questions, three of the five words are related in some way. Which two words do not belong with the three related words? Mark the correct words on the answer sheet.

31. collection   flowers   bunch   stamps   gathering

32. diminish   magnify   shrink   dwindle   divide

33.   authorise persist freedom permit allow

34.   turbulent thunderous raging subdued silent

35.   demolish construct destroy erect build

In the following questions, a different code is used for each question. The first word has been worked out for you. Work out the second word, using the same code. The alphabet is provided to help you. Mark the correct word on the answer sheet.

A B C D E F G H I J K L M N O P Q R S T U V W X Y Z

36.   If the code for SMALL is TLBKM what is the code for CROWD?

37.   If the code for SAFE is TCII what is the code for FAME?

38.   If the code for SCAR is UACP what does DPKK represent?

39.   If the code for RANT is QYKP what is the code for RMFH?

40.   If the code for DARE is XYZT what does ZTYX represent?

In the following questions, find the letters that complete the sentence in the most sensible way. The alphabet is provided to help you. Mark the correct letters on the answer sheet.

A B C D E F G H I J K L M N O P Q R S T U V W X Y Z

41.   DE is to FG as LM is to _____

42.   PQ is to NS as WX is to _____

43.   LM is to IP as OP is to _____

44.   BG is to XK as SV is to _____

45.   KM is to JN as TU is to _____

In the following questions, the three numbers in each group are related in the same way. Find the number that completes the last group. Mark the correct number on the answer sheet.

46.   5 (6) 11   7 (12) 19   8 ( ) 21

47.   17 (70) 18   37 (122) 24   18 ( ) 15

48.   68 (52) 18   76 (62) 24   48 ( ) 16

49.   17 (30) 43   37 (25) 13   16 ( ) 74

50.   9 (90) 5   8 (144) 9   12 ( ) 10

In the following questions, find the number that continues the series in the most sensible way. Mark the correct number on the answer sheet.

51.   2   7   23   72   220   _____

52.   720   144   36   12   6   _____

53.   5   7   12   19   31   50   _____

54.   8   9   11   12   15   16   20   21   _____

55.   29   28   27   24   24   19   20   _____

In the following questions, find the letter or letters that continue(s) the series in the most sensible way. The alphabet is provided to help you. Mark the correct letter(s) on the answer sheet.

A B C D E F G H I J K L M N O P Q R S T U V W X Y Z

56.   C   E   H   L   Q   _____

57.   W   V   T   Q   M   _____

58.   M   N   O   L   Q   J   S   _____

59.   FB   HD   JF   LH   _____

60.   D   D   E   G   J   N   _____

In the following questions, the words BOOTS, BOAST, TOAST, STABS, and BOATS have been coded into symbols. Match each set of symbols with its corresponding word. Mark the correct word on the answer sheet.

61.   ? □ ! x z

62.   x z ! ? x

63.   ? □ ! z x

64.   z □ ! x z

65.   John's father was 32 years old when John was born. John is now 10 years old. In how many years will John be exactly half his father's age?

In the following questions, one of the words from the bracket on the left can be joined to a word from the bracket on the right to form a completely new and proper word. Mark the two correct words on the answer sheet.

66. (CARPET HIDE HIGH)   (STAIR FITTING WAY)

67. (ENGINE IN PORT)   (POWER TEND CAR)

68. (CARE BE FORE)   (GIVE FULL AN)

69. (PLEA CRIME REST)   (GUILTY SURE ASSURED)

70. (CARD WARD STAR)   (PACK ACE ROBE)

In the following questions, find the two words, one from each set of brackets, that will complete the sentence in the most sensible way. Mark the correct words on the answer sheet.

71. Different is to (flavour, type, dissimilar) as identical is to (colour, appearance, matching).

72. Flexible is to (adaptable, light, electricity) as rigid is to (steel, harsh, stiff).

73. Delayed is to (weather, traffic, late) as punctual is to (time, jam, prompt).

74. Calm is to (relaxed, smooth, behaviour) as anxious is to (angry, mood, tense).

75. Gentle is to is to (generous, wind, kind) as severe is to (gale, punish, strict).

In the following questions, there are two pairs of words in brackets. Only one of the five answers will go equally well with both. Select the correct word and mark it on the answer sheet.

76. (order command)   (lead guide)
    dictate demand direct responsible military

77. (penalty charge)   (cloudless pleasant)
    punishment reward fine imposition assessment

78. (outstanding superb)   (colossal immense)
    achievement great brilliant diligent meritorious

79. (fair impartial)   (fair decent)
    tolerant unbiased respectful disciplined just

80. (portion section)   (guise role)
    fraction incomplete part responsible capacity

Anthem Test Papers
11+ and 12+ Verbal Reasoning Book 1
Answer Sheet 10

Please select your answers by filling in the correct boxes.

Name:

1
- degree ☐
- travel ☐
- map ☐
- direction ☐
- geography ☐

2
- uncertain ☐
- fake ☐
- false ☐
- cross ☐
- mark ☐

3
- reasonable ☐
- equipment ☐
- item ☐
- optional ☐
- necessary ☐

4
- notice ☐
- concern ☐
- eliminate ☐
- ignore ☐
- mistake ☐

5
- group ☐
- catalogue ☐
- scatter ☐
- form ☐
- trees ☐

6
- ignore ☐
- comfort ☐
- nurse ☐
- discuss ☐
- agree ☐
- argue ☐

7
- victory ☐
- overcome ☐
- army ☐
- star ☐
- entertainer ☐
- renowned ☐

8
- music ☐
- peace ☐
- loud ☐
- defence ☐
- yield ☐
- strike ☐

9
- referee ☐
- law ☐
- person ☐
- play ☐
- section ☐
- machine ☐

10
- abundant ☐
- food ☐
- drought ☐
- author ☐
- words ☐
- story ☐

11
- 17 ☐
- 25 ☐
- 26 ☐
- 34 ☐
- 36 ☐

12
- 24 ☐
- 34 ☐
- 38 ☐
- 70 ☐
- 120 ☐

13
- 22 ☐
- 30 ☐
- 34 ☐
- 44 ☐
- 66 ☐

14
- 8 ☐
- 19 ☐
- 25 ☐
- 42 ☐
- 58 ☐

15
- 16 ☐
- 32 ☐
- 36 ☐
- 49 ☐
- 60 ☐

16
- 81 ☐
- 108 ☐
- 135 ☐
- 162 ☐
- 243 ☐

17
- 27 ☐
- 75 ☐
- 40 ☐
- 35 ☐
- 20 ☐

18
- 42 ☐
- 43 ☐
- 44 ☐
- 45 ☐
- 46 ☐

19
- 3 ☐
- 10 ☐
- 15 ☐
- 20 ☐
- 23 ☐

20
- 37 ☐
- 38 ☐
- 39 ☐
- 48 ☐
- 75 ☐

21
- EYFN ☐
- EFFN ☐
- EYFM ☐
- EYFO ☐
- EYGN ☐

22
- DNYW ☐
- DNYU ☐
- DNXV ☐
- DNYV ☐
- DNWV ☐

23
- ROBE ☐
- ROAR ☐
- ROSE ☐
- ROUT ☐
- ROLE ☐

24
- CAGE ☐
- CALM ☐
- CAPE ☐
- CAFÉ ☐
- CAVE ☐

25
- BAKE ☐
- BAIL ☐
- BAND ☐
- BANG ☐
- BAIT ☐

26
- MO ☐
- MM ☐
- MN ☐
- NN ☐
- ON ☐

27
- MQ ☐
- NQ ☐
- PQ ☐
- NP ☐
- NR ☐

28
- GH ☐
- HI ☐
- GJ ☐
- GI ☐
- FI ☐

29
- RJ ☐
- RI ☐
- RH ☐
- SI ☐
- QI ☐

30
- WW ☐
- WU ☐
- WV ☐
- UV ☐
- WT ☐

31
- B ☐
- Y ☐
- R ☐
- T ☐
- N ☐

32
- S ☐
- E ☐
- K ☐
- T ☐
- P ☐

33
- S ☐
- M ☐
- L ☐
- R ☐
- P ☐

34
- D ☐
- S ☐
- L ☐
- T ☐
- P ☐

35
- P ☐
- D ☐
- K ☐
- T ☐
- Y ☐

36
- C ☐
- L ☐
- O ☐
- T ☐
- ☐

37
- B ☐
- O ☐
- A ☐
- S ☐
- T ☐

38
- C ☐
- A ☐
- R ☐
- D ☐
- ☐

39
- A ☐
- C ☐
- T ☐
- R ☐
- Y ☐

40
- C ☐
- A ☐
- S ☐
- T ☐
- E ☐

Answer Sheet 10

Please select your answers by filling in the correct boxes.

41
- The teacher ☐
- teacher took ☐
- five extra ☐
- extra pupils ☐
- the trip ☐

42
- Waste products ☐
- products are ☐
- are on ☐
- on the ☐
- the increase ☐

43
- was the ☐
- only cricket ☐
- cricket pitch ☐
- pitch in ☐
- India covered ☐

44
- The orders ☐
- orders given ☐
- given were ☐
- were simple ☐
- simple and ☐

45
- To make ☐
- make slap ☐
- slap into ☐
- into sap ☐
- remove the ☐

46
- SEE ☐
- PEN ☐
- REP ☐
- ARE ☐
- PEA ☐

47
- ATE ☐
- TEA ☐
- SET ☐
- SAT ☐
- EAT ☐

48
- RARE ☐
- HEAR ☐
- REAR ☐
- AREA ☐
- EACH ☐

49
- RAVE ☐
- RARE ☐
- ACRE ☐
- CAVE ☐
- RACE ☐

50
- TOP ☐
- MOP ☐
- POT ☐
- TOO ☐
- MAP ☐

51
- K ☐
- L ☐
- M ☐
- N ☐
- O ☐

52
- HI ☐
- HJ ☐
- HV ☐
- JV ☐
- IV ☐

53
- M ☐
- L ☐
- K ☐
- J ☐
- R ☐

54
- U ☐
- V ☐
- W ☐
- X ☐
- Y ☐

55
- HT ☐
- FS ☐
- HS ☐
- GS ☐
- HU ☐

56
- plead ☐
- expand ☐
- shrink ☐
- guilty ☐
- diminish ☐
- large ☐

57
- happy ☐
- elation ☐
- fringe ☐
- sad ☐
- despair ☐
- edge ☐

58
- boast ☐
- strange ☐
- injure ☐
- known ☐
- handicap ☐
- brag ☐

59
- devise ☐
- mix ☐
- courage ☐
- part ☐
- separate ☐
- bravery ☐

60
- still ☐
- movement ☐
- speed ☐
- rapid ☐
- motionless ☐
- reduce ☐

61
- LIT ☐
- LOG ☐
- LOW ☐
- SIP ☐
- GIN ☐

62
- PAL ☐
- AND ☐
- LAP ☐
- LOG ☐
- SIP ☐

63
- LAY ☐
- FOG ☐
- LOG ☐
- DID ☐
- BID ☐

64
- SAT ☐
- IMP ☐
- DID ☐
- SIT ☐
- SHE ☐

65
- PAD ☐
- MAD ☐
- MAN ☐
- MID ☐
- CAN ☐

66
- A ☐
- B ☐
- C ☐
- D ☐
- F ☐

67
- A ☐
- B ☐
- C ☐
- D ☐
- F ☐

68
- A ☐
- B ☐
- C ☐
- D ☐
- F ☐

69
- A ☐
- B ☐
- C ☐
- D ☐
- F ☐

70
- A ☐
- B ☐
- C ☐
- D ☐
- F ☐

71
- conceal ☐
- divulge ☐
- disguise ☐
- curtain ☐
- secret ☐
- reveal ☐

72
- ferocious ☐
- calm ☐
- punishment ☐
- disciplined ☐
- tame ☐
- sentence ☐

73
- dignified ☐
- exciting ☐
- party ☐
- frivolous ☐
- music ☐
- enjoymnet ☐

74
- stationary ☐
- flexible ☐
- precious ☐
- moving ☐
- heavy ☐
- fragile ☐

75
- neutral ☐
- palatial ☐
- referee ☐
- biased ☐
- fraction ☐
- decision ☐

76
- Alice ☐
- Betsie ☐
- Lily ☐
- Pat ☐
- Ted ☐

77
- 1 ☐
- 2 ☐
- 3 ☐
- 4 ☐
- 5 ☐

78
- Alice ☐
- Betsie ☐
- Lily ☐
- Pat ☐
- Ted ☐

79
- history ☐
- geography ☐
- maths ☐
- science ☐
- French ☐

80
- 1 ☐
- 2 ☐
- 3 ☐
- 4 ☐
- 5 ☐

Test Paper 10

In the following questions, there are two pairs of words. Only one of the five answers will go equally well with both pairs. Select the correct word and mark it on the answer sheet.

1. (bearing way)   (guidance control)
   degree travel map direction geography

2. (incorrect wrong)   (dishonest treacherous)
   uncertain fake false cross mark

3. (indispensible vital)   (crucial required)
   reasonable equipment item optional necessary

4. (disregard omit)   (neglect overlook)
   notice concern eliminate ignore mistake

5. (cluster assemble)   (band classify)
   group catalogue scatter form trees

In the following questions, find the two words, one from each set of brackets, that will complete the sentence in the most sensible way. Mark the correct words on the answer sheet.

6. Console is to (ignore, comfort, nurse) as dispute is to (discuss, agree, argue).

7. Conquer is to (victory, overcome, army) as famous is to (star, entertainer, renowned).

8. Noise is to (music, peace, loud) as resist is to (defence, yield, strike).

9. Judge is to (referee, law, person) as part is to (play, section, machine).

10. Plentiful is to (abundant, food, drought) as tale is to (author, words, story).

In the following questions, the three numbers in each group are related in the same way. Find the number that completes the last group. Mark the correct number on the answer sheet.

11. 5 (22) 6   7 (34) 10   8 ( ) 9

12. 8 (40) 10   6 (60) 20   10 ( ) 14

13. 8 (20) 4   10 (26) 6   12 ( ) 10

14. 20 (8) 3   44 (16) 7   36 ( ) 7

15. 8 (29) 5   7 (52) 9   6 ( ) 10

In the following questions, find the number that continues the series in the most sensible way. Mark the correct number on the answer sheet.

16. 2 1 6 3 18 9 54 27 _____

17. 120 111 100 99 80 87 60 _____

18. 9 14 20 27 35 _____

19. 9 9 11 7 13 5 15 _____

20. 21 30 27 36 33 42 _____

In the following questions, a different code is used for each question. The first word has been worked out for you. Work out the second word, using the same code. The alphabet is provided to help you. Mark the correct word on the answer sheet.

A B C D E F G H I J K L M N O P Q R S T U V W X Y Z

21. If the code for SUMS is RSJO what is the code for FAIR?

22. If the code for SING is QKLI what is the code for FLAT?

23. If the code for SORE is ABCD what does CBAD represent?

24. If the code for SHED is QFCB what does AYDC represent?

25. If the code for CARE is ZYQE what does YYHT represent?

In the following questions, find the letters that complete the sentence in the most sensible way. The alphabet is provided to help you. Mark the correct letters on the answer sheet.

A B C D E F G H I J K L M N O P Q R S T U V W X Y Z

26. BD is to EF as JL is to _____

27. KL is to JM as OP is to _____

28. RS is to OQ as JK is to _____

29. FG is to KB as MN is to _____

30. AZ is to BY as VW is to _____

In the questions below, the same letter must fit in both sets of brackets to complete the word in front of the brackets and begin the word after the brackets. Mark the correct letter on the answer sheet.

31.   BEE () EARLY   PLA () AIL

32.   PIN () HEM   SAIN () HUMB

33.   PEA () AID   TAL () EMON

34.   SEA () HOSE   POIN () RIP

35.   CAR () WIN   PAR () RICK

In the following questions, one letter can be moved from the word on the left to the word on the right to form two new words. The letter may be removed from any position in the first word and placed in any position in the second word. No other letters may be rearranged. Mark the correct letter on the answer sheet.

36.   CLOT   KNEE

37.   BOAST   PETS

38.   CARD   OWN

39.   FACTORY   FLING

40.   CASTE   GAP

In the following questions, a four-letter word can be formed from the letters at the end of one word and the beginning of the next, without changing the order of the letters. Find the pair of words and mark it on the answer sheet.

41.   The teacher took five extra pupils on the trip.

42.   Waste products are on the increase.

43.   It was the only cricket pitch in India covered in grass.

44.   The orders given were simple and clear.

45.   To make slap into sap remove the letter L.

In the following questions, there are three pairs of words. Find the word that completes the last pair of words in the same way as in the first two pairs. Mark the correct word on the answer sheet.

46.   CREATE CAT   : SLEETS SET   : PREENS _____

47.   PEAT   PET   : BEAT   BET   : SEAT   _____

48.   AREA   REAR   :   IDEA   DEAD   :   HARE   _____

49.   SCENT   SENT   :   SCORE   SORE   :   CRAVE   _____

50.   GRAVE   EAR   :   TRADE   EAR   :   STOMP   _____

In the following questions, find the letter or letters that continue(s) the series in the most sensible way. The alphabet is provided to help you. Mark the correct letter(s) on the answer sheet.

A B C D E F G H I J K L M N O P Q R S T U V W X Y Z

51.   B   D   F   H   J   _____

52.   DZ   EY   FX   GW   _____

53.   C   W   E   U   G   S   I   Q   _____

54.   H   I   K   N   R   _____

55.   PK   NM   LO   JQ   _____

In the following questions, find the two words, one from each set of brackets, that are the closest in meaning. Mark the correct words on the answer sheet.

56.   (plead, expand, shrink)   (guilty, diminish, large)

57.   (happy, elation, fringe)   (sad, despair, edge)

58.   (boast, strange, injure)   (known, handicap, brag)

59.   (devise, mix, courage)   (part, separate, bravery)

60.   (still, movement, speed)   (rapid, motionless, reduce)

In the following questions, the letters in capitals are missing three consecutive letters that can be inserted into the capital letters to form a word that completes the sentence. The three consecutive letters themselves form a sensible word. Mark the missing three-letter word on the answer sheet.

61.   The wind was BING the letter across the playground.

62.   The audience enthusiastically CPED the performance.

63.   The boy ate a KIRAM of sweets.

64.   He HEATED before jumping off the diving board.

65.   The naughty pupil was REPRIDED by the headmaster.

In the following questions, A = 10, B = 5, C = 2, D = 4, and F = 8. Work out the values of the following, giving your answer as a letter. Mark the correct letter on the answer sheet.

66.   C × D

67. $\dfrac{A}{B}$

68. $\dfrac{A \times D}{B}$

69.   CB – C

70.   CF ÷ (D ÷ C)

In the following questions, select the two words, one from each set of brackets, that are the most opposite in meaning. Mark the correct words on the answer sheet.

71.   (conceal, divulge, disguise)   (curtain, secret, reveal)

72.   (ferocious, calm, punishment)   (disciplined, tame, sentence)

73.   (dignified, exciting, party)   (frivolous, music, enjoyment)

74.   (stationary, flexible, precious)   (moving, heavy, fragile)

75.   (neutral, palatial, referee)   (biased, fraction, decision)

Alice, Betsie, Lily, Pat and Ted were asked whether they enjoyed history, geography, maths, science and French. Alice and Pat said they enjoyed history, whilst Betsie and Ted said they enjoyed geography only. Betsie and Ted did not enjoy maths but both enjoyed science. Lily enjoyed maths and French. For the following questions, mark the correct answer on the answer sheet.

76.   Who enjoyed the same two subjects as Alice?

77.   How many children enjoyed both geography and science?

78.   Who enjoyed French but not science?

79.   What is the most popular subject?

80.   How many lessons did Lily and Pat enjoy together?

Answers to Test Papers

Test 1 Answers

1.	mark		41.	ENDLESS
2.	object		42.	CAREFREE
3.	rock		43.	LESSON
4.	present		44.	CUPBOARD
5.	piece		45.	BEHAVE
6.	noise & silence		46.	eject & patch
7.	knowledge & ignorance		47.	cruel & whole
8.	leader & follower		48.	hate & encourage
9.	present & past		49.	metre & century
10.	fake & real		50.	two & three
11.	E		51.	walk & crawl
12.	L		52.	precede & winner
13.	B		53.	lucky & looking
14.	R		54.	measure & weigh
15.	E		55.	pain & punish
16.	UW		56.	that escaped
17.	LR		57.	the choir
18.	CD		58.	each entrant
19.	YZ		59.	players hopping
20.	MO		60.	boys lowers
21.	63		61.	T
22.	1440		62.	A
23.	21		63.	FO
24.	66		64.	Y
25.	805		65.	L
26.	POLE		66.	SINK
27.	MARE		67.	JULY
28.	REAL		68.	DTGCF
29.	RAW		69.	IMCJ
30.	MOAN		70.	FDUH
31.	P		71.	deluge & flood
32.	H		72.	colossal & massive
33.	W		73.	clamour & noise
34.	L		74.	honour & respect
35.	K		75.	rebel & mutiny
36.	WANE		76.	ALL
37.	RENT		77.	TOO
38.	TUBE		78.	PAD
39.	RAID		79.	ANT
40.	PACT		80.	PEA

Test 2 Answers

1.	B		41.	RACES
2.	E		42.	SCARE
3.	B		43.	CASES
4.	Y		44.	EASES
5.	T		45.	CARES
6.	27		46.	PLATFORM
7.	33		47.	SEAGULL
8.	12		48.	CANNOT
9.	360		49.	BEGIN
10.	21		50.	CAPSIZE
11.	CREW		51.	Y
12.	BEEN		52.	G
13.	TALE		53.	P
14.	PEER		54.	T
15.	SOAP		55.	E
16.	area & interior		56.	Alas the
17.	timidity & cowardice		57.	name and
18.	demolish & raze		58.	left his
19.	public & open		59.	Bottles and
20.	intensity & heighten		60.	discovers old
21.	SNVME		61.	cabbage & vegetable
22.	SPEED		62.	puppy & dog
23.	CQDX		63.	rung & ladder
24.	CART		64.	frown & cross
25.	ZYYX		65.	funnel & ship
26.	NO		66.	robust & strong
27.	SV		67.	help & aid
28.	UZ		68.	bright & shining
29.	SQ		69.	peculiar & strange
30.	OZ		70.	feeble & weak
31.	13		71.	U
32.	7		72.	X
33.	66		73.	V
34.	40		74.	W
35.	45		75.	X
36.	W		76.	OUR
37.	H		77.	LAP
38.	H		78.	END
39.	H		79.	LAY
40.	K		80.	ATE

Test 3 Answers

1.	TALE		41.	HAT
2.	RIND		42.	CAT
3.	KIND		43.	BATS
4.	SKY		44.	DONE
5.	RAILS		45.	BAT
6.	U		46.	ONE
7.	U		47.	OUR
8.	F		48.	TEN
9.	W		49.	RAT
10.	KU		50.	CAT
11.	27		51.	two odd
12.	3600		52.	favourite story
13.	100		53.	There are
14.	11		54.	The ape
15.	44		55.	Time and
16.	REAR		56.	selected & time
17.	RACE		57.	sailed & the
18.	RARE		58.	number & hung
19.	ACRE		59.	park & were
20.	9.15am		60.	Broke & after
21.	H		61.	force
22.	I		62.	mark
23.	N		63.	part
24.	C		64.	record
25.	I		65.	break
26.	Bill		66.	65
27.	Fred		67.	75
28.	train		68.	18
29.	1		69.	18
30.	Pat		70.	40
31.	E		71.	piano & violin
32.	N		72.	head & hair
33.	B		73.	carpenter & nail
34.	P		74.	enter & occupy
35.	W		75.	part & keep
36.	pork & beef		76.	X
37.	hand & foot		77.	Y
38.	whisper & walk		78.	P
39.	shell & rind		79.	B
40.	July & May		80.	Y

Test 4 Answers

1. BREAKFAST
2. CARPET
3. NOTHING
4. ACTOR
5. TABLECLOTH
6. SENDER
7. ECHO
8. EASE
9. DEED
10. MALE
11. PLUM
12. SCORE
13. PAIN
14. SCORE
15. FIVE
16. 3
17. 32
18. 11
19. 23
20. 60
21. ra<u>re st</u>amps
22. th<u>e mo</u>untains
23. pi<u>e re</u>mains
24. missin<u>g rin</u>g
25. you<u>r an</u>ger
26. rare & unusual
27. forgive & pardon
28. part & fraction
29. cherish & love
30. foggy & misty
31. audience & congregation
32. doubt & knowledge
33. sorrow & failure
34. enormous & huge
35. radio & television
36. PIN
37. OUR
38. PEA
39. PAR
40. NOW

41. E
42. F
43. P
44. C
45. N
46. 12
47. 23
48. 15
49. 63
50. 75
51. WX
52. VU
53. LK
54. XV
55. QSU
56. A
57. D
58. E
59. E
60. A
61. Bill
62. John
63. Peter
64. Ann
65. Joan
66. cross
67. ditch
68. box
69. power
70. smart
71. JK
72. LI
73. NS
74. UQ
75. OG
76. actual
77. enlarge
78. wrath
79. rush
80. distant

Test 5 Answers

1.	W	43.	LINE	
2.	R		LINT	
3.	Y	44.	TIME	
4.	T		TIDE	
5.	R	45.	FIST	
6.	K		MIST	
7.	F	46.	MOONLIGHT	
8.	E	47.	BLACKBERRY	
9.	G	48.	THUNDERBOLT	
10.	T	49.	BEEHIVE	
11.	PR	50.	ROSEBUD	
12.	TS	51.	finger & thumb	
13.	DW	52.	fright & scare	
14.	WE	53.	collapse & fall	
15.	ED	54.	enemy & foe	
16.	rough & smooth	55.	pretty & attractive	
17.	fake & real	56.	1052	
18.	relaxed & tense	57.	2503	
19.	come & go	58.	0351	
20.	jittery & calm	59.	0503	
21.	is now	60.	7	
22.	panic ensued	61.	ball	
23.	threw ink	62.	abandon	
24.	The naughty	63.	act	
25.	white markings	64.	charge	
26.	easy & late	65.	part	
27.	finish & undo	66.	4	
28.	failure & smooth	67.	44	
29.	serious & sink	68.	50	
30.	tumble & crowded	69.	24	
31.	RHMF	70.	486	
32.	FOUL	71.	WASP	
33.	TDXT	72.	CARP	
34.	SKIN	73.	FILM	
35.	HJQU	74.	TILE	
36.	23	75.	FORM	
37.	30	76.	pier & harbour	
38.	36	77.	uncle & father	
39.	32	78.	lead & iron	
40.	14	79.	world & earth	
41.	SANE	80.	bones & blood	
	SANG			
42.	DOLL			
	DULL			

Test 6 Answers

1.	T		41.	RTKOG
2.	T		42.	SCRAP
3.	E		43.	MACE
4.	N		44.	MADE
5.	U		45.	SHOP
6.	date & day		46.	H
7.	circle & perimeter		47.	W
8.	slender & minute		48.	T
9.	hide & capture		49.	N
10.	adventure & accident		50.	L
11.	NG		51.	REAPS
12.	P		52.	SPARE
13.	PKN		53.	PEARS
14.	KG		54.	SPEAR
15.	YX		55.	185
16.	crab and		56.	28
17.	Pupils often		57.	44
18.	Apples and		58.	21
19.	The room		59.	7
20.	candles shone		60.	23
21.	fear & sadness		61.	F
22.	eight & twelve		62.	F
23.	sad & funny		63.	A
24.	caught & bought		64.	D
25.	window & door		65.	D
26.	READ		66.	frugal & extravagant
27.	ROAD		67.	courageous & cowardly
28.	STIR		68.	mock & encourage
29.	RED		69.	possible & improbable
30.	PIT		70.	mourn & rejoice
31.	48		71.	delay & postpone
32.	82		72.	calm & mild
33.	77		73.	hastily & speedily
34.	104		74.	demolish & destroy
35.	107		75.	evade & avoid
36.	ZY		76.	holidaymakers & crowded
37.	IX		77.	pupils & lesson
38.	WF		78.	coach & group
39.	NL		79.	days & sun
40.	MY		80.	waves & yacht

Test 7 Answers

1.	ROTTEN		41.	B
2.	MANAGE		42.	E
3.	STABBED		43.	D
4.	NOTHING		44.	A
5.	JUSTICE		45.	C
6.	FADE		46.	water & food
7.	SPOKE		47.	healthy & strong
8.	TOLD		48.	fruit & fuel
9.	FOUR		49.	cease & stop
10.	APPLE		50.	palm & sole
11.	a cheap		51.	hard & solid
12.	coloured umbrellas		52.	fatigue & weariness
13.	working rowers		53.	melt & thaw
14.	apple adds		54.	outcome & result
15.	watch attentively		55.	attack & assault
16.	NO		56.	dark & bright
17.	PK		57.	pond & lake
18.	GI		58.	two & four
19.	WF		59.	cold & warm
20.	GF		60.	today & tomorrow
21.	FIT		61.	ARM
22.	HARE		62.	GET
23.	BULB		63.	EVE
24.	INN		64.	NET
25.	DUST		65.	BAT
26.	P		66.	L
27.	J		67.	D
28.	FE		68.	H
29.	KX		69.	E
30.	DE		70.	O
31.	27		71.	M
32.	80		72.	T
33.	126		73.	B
34.	3		74.	E
35.	1		75.	P
36.	50		76.	miserly & generous
37.	28		77.	base & summit
38.	40		78.	decline & increase
39.	40		79.	confuse & clarify
40.	4		80.	care & neglect

Test 8 Answers

1.	PATTERN		41.	HNBS
2.	SOON		42.	NAME
3.	FEATHER		43.	OKPG
4.	DONOR		44.	FOOT
5.	FITTEST		45.	FOOD
6.	96		46.	above & beneath
7.	47		47.	real & imaginary
8.	16		48.	near & distant
9.	18		49.	quiet & noisy
10.	13		50.	cruelty & kindness
11.	OIL		51.	N
12.	ARE		52.	T
13.	BOAT		53.	B
14.	FIST		54.	W
15.	WINE		55.	L
16.	I		56.	scarf
17.	E		57.	decide
18.	B		58.	earth
19.	R		59.	villa
20.	T		60.	certainty
21.	woman & man		61.	23
22.	team & choir		62.	30
23.	stem & trunk		63.	36
24.	tenth & twentieth		64.	32
25.	liquid & distance		65.	56
26.	FOIL		66.	QR
27.	LUTE		67.	IN
28.	RAIL		68.	HW
29.	SLOW		69.	PV
30.	LAND		70.	HG
31.	not every		71.	clap
32.	The athlete		72.	cross
33.	she do		73.	erect
34.	idea rejected		74.	game
35.	come at		75.	mark
36.	P		76.	entertain & amuse
37.	J		77.	fearless & courageous
38.	W		78.	group & collection
39.	NO		79.	jealous & envious
40.	TQ		80.	protect & safeguard

Test 9 Answers

1.	REST	41.	NO
2.	TASK	42.	UZ
3.	PAST	43.	LS
4.	MATE	44.	OZ
5.	SAME	45.	SV
6.	AND	46.	13
7.	TEN	47.	66
8.	END	48.	40
9.	TEN	49.	45
10.	THE	50.	240
11.	B	51.	665
12.	T	52.	6
13.	K	53.	81
14.	L	54.	26
15.	H	55.	13
16.	L	56.	W
17.	E	57.	H
18.	G	58.	H
19.	E	59.	NJ
20.	S	60.	S
21.	sells kippers	61.	BOAST
22.	discover aids	62.	STABS
23.	calm endless	63.	BOATS
24.	post early	64.	TOAST
25.	The report	65.	22
26.	colossal & minute	66.	HIGHWAY
27.	threaten & protect	67.	INTEND
28.	distress & comfort	68.	BEAN
29.	polite & discourteous	69.	PLEASURE
30.	increase & deduct	70.	WARDROBE
31.	flowers & stamps	71.	dissimilar & matching
32.	magnify & divide	72.	adaptable & stiff
33.	persist & freedom	73.	late & prompt
34.	subdued & silent	74.	relaxed & tense
35.	demolish & destroy	75.	kind & strict
36.	DQPVE	76.	direct
37.	GCPI	77.	fine
38.	BRIM	78.	great
39.	SOIL	79.	just
40.	READ	80.	part

Test 10 Answers

1. direction
2. false
3. necessary
4. ignore
5. group
6. comfort & argue
7. overcome & renowned
8. peace & yield
9. referee & section
10. abundant & story
11. 34
12. 70
13. 34
14. 12
15. 49
16. 162
17. 75
18. 44
19. 3
20. 39
21. EYFN
22. DNYV
23. ROSE
24. CAFE
25. BAIT
26. MN
27. NQ
28. GI
29. RI
30. WV
31. N
32. T
33. L
34. T
35. T
36. L
37. S
38. D
39. Y
40. E

41. extra pupils
42. Waste products
43. pitch in
44. simple and
45. slap into
46. PEN
47. SET
48. AREA
49. CAVE
50. POT
51. L
52. HV
53. K
54. W
55. HS
56. shrink & diminish
57. fringe & edge
58. boast & brag
59. courage & bravery
60. still & motionless
61. LOW
62. LAP
63. LOG
64. SIT
65. MAN
66. F
67. C
68. F
69. F
70. F
71. conceal & reveal
72. ferocious & tame
73. dignified & frivolous
74. stationary & moving
75. neutral & biased
76. Pat
77. 2
78. Lily
79. maths
80. 1

ANTHEM LEARNING BOOKS	
TITLE	ISBN
Anthem How To Do 11 + and 12+Verbal Reasoning:Technique and Practice	ISBN13: 978 0 85728 382 5 ISBN 10: 0 85728 382 0
Anthem Test Papers 11 + and 12+Verbal Reasoning Book 1	ISBN13: 978 0 85728 383 2 ISBN10: 0 85728 383 9
Anthem Test Papers 11 + and 12+Verbal Reasoning Book 2	ISBN13: 978 0 85728 385 6 ISBN 10: 0 85728 385 5
Anthem Short Revision Papers 11 + and 12+Verbal Reasoning Book 1	ISBN13: 978 0 85728 384 9 ISBN10: 0 85728 384 7
Anthem Short Revision Papers 11 + and 12+Verbal Reasoning Book 2	ISBN13: 978 0 85728 386 3 ISBN10: 0 85728 386 3

Anthem Junior English Book Preparatory Book	ISBN13: 978 0 85728 356 6 ISBN10: 0 85728 356 1
Anthem Junior English Book 1	ISBN13: 978 0 85728 358 0 ISBN10: 0 85728 358 8
Anthem Junior English Book 2	ISBN13: 978 0 85728 360 3 ISBN10: 0 85728 360 X
Anthem Junior English Book 3	ISBN13: 978 0 85728 362 7 ISBN10: 0 85728 362 6
Anthem English Book 1	ISBN13: 978 0 85728 364 1 ISBN10: 0 85728 364 2
Anthem English Book 2	ISBN13: 978 0 85728 366 5 ISBN10: 0 85728 366 9
Anthem English Book 3	ISBN13: 978 0 85728 368 9 ISBN10: 0 85728 368 5

Anthem Junior Mathematics Book 3	ISBN13: 978 0 85728 370 2 ISBN10: 0 85728 370 7
Anthem Junior Mathematics Book 3 Test Papers	ISBN13: 978 0 85728 372 6 ISBN10: 0 85728 372 3
Anthem Mathematics Book 1	ISBN13: 978 0 85728 373 3 ISBN10: 0 85728 373 1
Anthem Mathematics Book 1 Test Papers	ISBN13: 978 0 85728 375 7 ISBN10: 0 85728 375 8
Anthem Mathematics Book 2	ISBN13: 978 0 85728 376 4 ISBN10: 0 85728 376 6
Anthem Mathematics Book 2 Test Papers	ISBN13: 978 0 85728 378 8 ISBN10: 0 85728 378 2
Anthem Mathematics Book 3	ISBN13: 978 0 85728 379 5 ISBN10: 0 85728 379 0
Anthem Mathematics Book 3 Test Papers	ISBN13: 978 0 85728 381 8 ISBN10: 0 85728 381 2

VISIT WWW.ANTHEMPRESS.COM TO ORDER ONLINE.

Printed in Great Britain
by Amazon

54173935R00056